A SHED, CHICKENS, SIENCYN AND ME

*A delightfully light humorous book set in a 1930s
South Wales valley*

Edwina Slack

CONTENTS

INTRODUCTION

"*A Shed, Chickens, Siencyn and Me*" is a delightfully light humorous book set in a 1930s South Wales valley. It is written through the perceptive eyes of a young girl, Megan and it is where we meet her family and the characters of the village, such as, Mrs Hughes News, Mr William Lewis Amen, Selwyn the Psalms, Auntie Scissors Ann, a girl with pimples and a sniffle and Megan's favourite, - Siencyn Oddjobs (pronounced "Shenkin"; as there is no "J" for Jenkins in the Welsh alphabet)!

Siencyn lived in a shed on the side of a hill; this was good for three things, to look after his chickens, to tend his allotment and to keep away from his wife. He smoked OP's (other peoples), never complained and always got out of trouble with a smile and a wink. He was not on time for work one morning and when caught slopping off early in the afternoon his boss shouted, "Mr Jenkins, bearing in mind what time you arrived this morning, what time do you call this to be leaving?" He replied, "I know, but I don't want to be late twice in one day, now do I?"

The language and attitudes are typically South Walian and each chapter is its' own adventure with Siencyn in there somewhere causing mayhem. Megan's awareness, sensitivity and intelligence are obvious through her lyrical narrative and while we enjoy her innocence, "*and the Policeman muttered and mumbled, and once I thought he said a naughty word, but I must have been mistaken. Policemen don't say language*", her engaging writing style provides the reader with many different levels of insight and the hugely entertaining bigger picture, is there to be enjoyed.

1

Mam, and her sometimes acerbic sister Aunty "Scissors" Ann cross swords with Siencyn in many odd and unusual ways, and while it's quite hard to see who actually gets the upper hand, in the end they call it a truce, "there's no harm in old Siencyn", as Megan's "Dadda", always says and Siencyn comes to live with the family. It's full of 1930s values, the wit of the Welsh and a touch of nostalgia.

While the back drop of these stories are the Hungry Thirties and poverty was palpable, the stories are told with a depth of humour which leaves the reader with a smile on their face, a lighter heart and a just a small tear just in the corner of one eye.

The last chapter of the appendix though, is not to be taken lightly. It's not a Siencyn tale but a social commentary from the authors' childhood that completes the picture of a 1930s Welsh valley. The memory puts all the stories into context and while it's a powerful chapter on its own, it adds weight to the tales of Siencyn and the characters of the village become alive and closer to the reader.

David C.L. Slack

CHAPTER 1

THE CRIME OF THE CENTURY

It was the talk of the place when Siencyn Oddjobs got the Insurance money after his old Aunty from Swansea left this Vale of Tears. She had fallen off a ladder while she was watching over the garden wall, in case the neighbour next door was cutting her privet hedge as well as pruning their own laurels.

Nobody would have thought he'd spent the money buying week-old chicks. Three dozen he bought from Mr Williams Mafondy and he told everybody he was going in for the egg business. He had ambitions to be a business tycoon, like American men in the pictures. The chickens would lay eggs, then hatch them, and he'd end up with thousands and thousands of chickens, and millions and millions of eggs. Sadly it was not to be.

First thing that went wrong was that the chickens was cockerels. Mr Williams Mafondy said nobody said nothing about wanting hens, only about wanting brown chickens. Siencyn said he ought to have understood he wanted brown chickens to give brown eggs!

Siencyn had to leave the eggs idea and go into the fattening for Christmas side of the business. That's when the second thing went wrong. The Insurance money didn't stretch to wire netting, and when the chickens was let out of the cwtch as they grew bigger, they got out of the run easy. It wasn't a very good run, only old pieces of corrugated iron, old iron bedsteads and a big metal panel with 'Sunlight Soap' on it in letters two foot high. The chickens got through the gap in the bedsteads, up the bank and on to the railway line and got their selves run over by the trains. After nearly half a dozen had been lost like that, Siencyn's wife Marged called him a proper old flag, sold the rest of the chickens back to Williams Mafondy, and put the money in the Post Office. Siencyn's heart was broke.

We met him the next day when Dadda and me was on our way to the allotment to cut a cabbage for Mam. He was leaning over his bailey wall looking real miserable.

"*Swmai* Siencyn, 'ow be?" asked Dadda.

"Oh, middling, middling," he answered. "I don't half miss my chickens though. If it wasn't for Marged and the Great Western Railway I'd be a rich man today, a real business typhoon."

Dadda said, "Why don't you apply for an allotment, keep your mind off your troubles like?"

"No thank you," said Siencyn. "I don't want no old allotment." He looked as if the world was a place of sorrow, and he was carrying the lot. Then he turned to me. "Well, *merch i*, what did you learn in school today?"

"We did History," I said. "And we learned all about a Ty-Un-Nos."

"Well now," said Siencyn. "Well, well, well. That little gel's got an 'ead on her shoulders. Go far she will. Tell us about it then."

"Well," I said. "Miss Thomas said that in Olden Days poor people couldn't afford to buy land to build a house, so if they found a place where no-one could see them and if they worked all night from sunset to sunrise and built a house, and had a fire lit and smoke coming from the chimney by dawn, then it was their very own house, and nobody could turn them out. That's what it means see, a House of One Night, in Welsh."

Siencyn scratched his head. "Tell me about it again," he said. So I did.

"And they couldn't be turned out?"

"No," I told him. "Miss Thomas said that the owner of the land could do nothing about it. But they had to have a fire lit in the fireplace, with smoke coming out of the chimney. If the bailiff caught them before it was finished, it wasn't legal. Then we had singing," I added.

But Siencyn wasn't interested in singing. "*Jawch*, I never knew that," he said. "Did you Mr Williams?"

"No, but if Teacher said it, it must be right. Teacher's been to College, so she knows. Well we got to be going. So long Siencyn." And off we went.

Siencyn met me coming from school the next day.

"That Ty-Un-Nos was all legal, wasn't it?" he asked, but I wasn't interested.

"We had sums today, and I had ten out of ten."

"*Ach-y-fi*. Old sums," he said, and went off up the road, his hands in his pockets, his eyes staring at the pavement.

We didn't see Siencyn for a bit after that, although we passed his house on the way to the allotment and saw Mrs Siencyn Oddjobs beating the mats and cleaning the windows. Then about two weeks later we saw him pushing a hand cart under the railway bridge that led past the allotments to a short cut to the colliery and the old quarry.

"Well, Well," said Dadda. "In the transport business now, is it?"

"What do you think of it Mr Williams?" said Siencyn, grinning all over his face. "Made the cart myself, I did."

It was a lovely cart. It had one yellow wheel, and the other wheel was off an old bicycle, and it had handles painted blue with 'Bracchi's Pure Ices' printed on them. The cart was full of pieces of wood, and a door with a frosted glass panel with 'Public' on it.

"What you got there?" asked Dadda.

"Lovely door, isn't it?" said Siencyn. "Mr Morgan the Red Cow is having new doors to the Public Bar. There was a bit of an accident there the other night with a couple of chairs and Fred Price's head, so no more glass no more, said Mr Morgan. He's sick of putting new glass in, and frosted glass is dear. So he's give me this door - the one that wasn't broken, like see. Real brass knob too."

"Where you going with all that?" asked Dadda.

"Can't stop, Mr Williams - in a 'urry like." And he was gone, pushing his barrow bumpety, bumpety, over the cobble stones.

When we got home, we told Mam about it while we was having tea.

"I've never in all my born days seen Siencyn move so fast," said Dadda.

"He's up to something, mark my words," said Mam. "What his poor wife do have to put up with, only the Dear Lord and the Chapel Sisterhood do know. A martyr that woman is, a regular martyr."

"Oh, there's no harm in old Siencyn," said Dadda.

"Isn't there?" said Mam. "I got my own opinion about that. All I hopes is he's not getting up to no good with them chickens again."

And then, about three weeks later, just when it was nearly time to break up from school for the August holidays, we had real excitement. It was just like in the pictures: crime, and the police, and what time did it all happen? and everything. It was a Wednesday, so most women went to Ponty Market. Marged Siencyn Oddjobs always went by eleven o'clock to meet her sister from Abercynon outside the Town Hall. They used to do their shopping, have a lovely faggots and peas dinner in the market, and then Mrs Siencyn

Oddjobs' sister used to catch the three o'clock bus back to Abercynon.

When Mrs Oddjobs got home by half past three - she'd been burgled!

Real burglars! It was all round the place in no time. Mrs Evans Risca heard her screaming, and called Sal next door, and then they ran in and then Mrs Evans put the kettle on to make tea to calm Mrs Oddjobs down, while Sal ran down to Foundry Road to get the police. The policeman was having five minutes, but he put his boots on and was on the scene in no time. Soon as I got home from school, Mam put a teisen lap and a pound of sugar in her basket and we went round to help.

It was just like Hollywood! Mrs Oddjobs crying in the middle room, with all the neighbours drinking tea and steam coming out of the back kitchen as they kept putting the kettle on. The Policeman was so big, his helmet nearly touched the ceiling. It was frightening, and I wouldn't have missed it for worlds. They was making a list of all the things that had gone - two horse hair chairs from the front room, a new rag rug, only finished six months ago, the table from the middle room, two pictures, 'Bear ye one another's burdens,' and 'Where your treasure is, there will your heart be also,' and a Text, 'Thou God see-est me.'

"Why would a burglar take the text?" asked Sal. "I'd have thought it would be the last thing he'd want to pinch."

"P'haps he's a religious maniac," said another woman, whose hair was standing on end with excitement and a new perm.

Then there was the bed from the back bedroom, with all the blankets and pillows, and a patchwork quilt made by Mrs Oddjobs' nephew's wife's mother, the little kettle, two chairs from the back kitchen, and a fox in a glass case. The discovery that the burglars had even taken the valance off the mantelpiece in the front room - red velvet with bobbles - made Mrs Oddjobs burst into tears again, and we was glad to have a slice of teisen lap and another cup of tea.

Suddenly Mrs Oddjobs remembered something.

"My husband!" she screamed. "Where's my husband? He was supposed to stay in and mind the house while I was out!"

"There's no sign of a struggle," said the Policeman. "No bloodstains anywhere. Stand back, while I search out the back."

The thought that Siencyn Oddjobs might have been murdered by burglars and thrown into his own nettles and chicken run was terrifying. We all watched from the back kitchen window, so as not to spoil the clues, but there was no sign of a body nowhere.

I can't remember who started the rumour that perhaps Siencyn had been kidnapped, but by eight o'clock all the neighbourhood was waiting for a ransom note, and views on how to raise the money was bandied about.

Some favoured a raffle, but as most of us was Chapel, a Celebrity Concert seemed the best idea. There hadn't been such excitement for years.

The Policeman suggested that the ladies had all better go home and let Mrs Oddjobs rest, while he went to get in touch with the rest of the Force at Ponty.

"Spoilsport," muttered Sal, but here comes Billy, the Policeman's son to say that his supper was ready, so telling us that he had better have a word on the telephone with his sergeant, he went off at a spanking rate. Mrs Thomas next door was sent to the chipshop for six cutlets and a tail, and seven penn'orth of chips, so between enjoying the supper, seeing where everything had been before it was stolen, and telling all the new people that turned up all about it, it was no time before the Policeman was back, with tomato sauce on his moustache.

"There's no more we can do tonight," he said. "It's dark and it's drizzling heavy, so tomorrow I'll crack the case."

Nobody really wanted to go home, but Mam suddenly remembered I should have been in bed hours ago. Just as we was going out the front door, here comes Dadda up the path.

"Oh No!" said Mam. "I never heard the pit hooter, and there's no supper and no water for his bath ready, and him tired out after his shift!"

Dadda, black with coal dust, was talking to the Policeman.

"What's the fuss about?" he was saying. "Half the women in the auction buzzing round here like bees after honey, and the men home from the pit these ten minutes and no food ready."

"It's Old Oddjobs," said the Policeman. "His house have been burgled and we can't find hair nor hide of him. Foul play cannot be ruled out."

"Foul play is it?" said Dadda, "He looked all right to me when I saw him this afternoon."

"But you've been down the pit since two o'clock," said the Policeman. "You're on the two to ten shift. How could you have seen him?"

"Well I come up with Tom Thomas - he broke his leg in two places - and I saw him into the Ambulance with the other Ambulance men. As I looked down the road to see them off like, there was old Siencyn passing, pushing that old barrow of his. He was managing all right then."

"What was on the barrow?" asked the Policeman. I wondered if it was going to the third degree like in the pictures, with James Cagney.

"Well," said Dadda. "I couldn't see much, he'd got it all covered over with a big rag rug, but it looked like furniture to me."

There was a scream from Mrs Oddjobs, who heard what Dadda had said.

"I'll kill him," she shouted. "I'll wring his neck! He's the one pinched my nice things. Where is he? Where's he gone? Let me get at him!"

"Now, now," said the Policeman. "We mustn't jump to conclusions."

"I'll jump to what I like," yelled Mrs Oddjobs. She was screaming and crying all together, so Sal and Mrs Evans took her inside to pacify her, and somebody mentioned Brandy, and all the women went back into the house so as not to miss nothing.

The Policeman wiped his forehead with his handkerchief. "This have been a day," he said. "I wonder what the old fool is up to."

"I'd like to know where he've got to," chuckled Dadda.

Suddenly, I said, "I know where he is."

"Husht," said Mam. "You don't know no such thing. Come on, it's long past your bedtime and I'm taking you home."

"Wait a minute," said Dadda. "Do you really think you know? You been in school all day."

"I didn't see him," I admitted. "But I expect he've gone to take his furniture to the Ty-Un-Nos he've been building this last fortnight."

"What's all this?" said the Policeman, looking stern at me, so I had to tell him about our History lesson in school, and how Siencyn had been doing things to the old shed that Meredith Jones had used to keep farm things in, up by the old quarry. He'd been pushing his old barrow up there, and I'd seen him. I suddenly remembered that Mam said I wasn't to go anywhere near the old quarry to play, but it was too late to stop now.

"Could you show me where it is?" asked the Policeman.

"No she couldn't," said Mam, real cross with me. "It's time she was in bed."

"I'm sorry Mrs Williams," said the Policeman. "But I've got to find out if Siencyn is all right, and if he've really taken them things. Come along little girl, it won't take long."

"She 'aven't got her wellingtons on," said Mam. "Only her daps, and she've got nothing for her head. Get her death of cold she will in this rain, at this time of night."

"I'll see to that," said the Policeman, and in no time at all I was wearing an old felt hat belonging to Mrs Oddjobs and I was being carried piggy back by the Policeman hisself.

We started off up the muddy path, the Policeman carrying me, then Dadda, then Mam coming behind. The rain was steady and the earth smelled sweet in the darkness, as I told the Policeman which way to go. After we'd passed just above the pit, we came to the little road that led to the old quarry. It was slippery with the rain, and very stony, and I didn't like holding on to the Policeman's neck. I wished Dadda would have carried me, but Mam wouldn't let me go near his pit clothes. Dadda shone the big torch on to the path, but they was all stumbling and sliding and the Policeman muttered and mumbled, and once I thought he said a naughty word, but I must have been mistaken. Policemen don't say language.

We turned a sharp corner by a big patch of brambles, and there we saw it, a dark shape of a shed, with a pale light at the window, and a few wisps of smoke coming out of a wobbly chimney.

"That's it," I cried. "That's Siencyn's new house!"

The Policeman put me down, and we went quietly up to the door. In the light of the torch, we could see that it had the word 'PUBLIC' on it, in frosted glass, and a handle about eighteen inches from the ground, and rough saw marks on the bottom edge where Siencyn must have cut the tall door to fit the short doorway.

The Policeman coughed important, and banged on the wooden bit of the door. "Open up," he shouted. "Come on now, we know you are in there!"

A dim light came close to the window, and Oddjobs face appeared between lace curtains. He nodded, and disappeared, and the door was thrown open. Gusts of smoke came out like a black cloud, and we all started to cough, and our eyes was stinging terrible. Siencyn stood on his doorstep, holding an oil lamp in his hand - that's one thing Mrs Oddjobs didn't know he'd taken, I thought.

"It's all right! It's legal," said Siencyn happily. "It's all legal! I got the fire lit and the smoke coming out of the chimney. Come you in, all of you, come and see what I done!"

Coughing, with tears running out of our eyes, we followed him in. By the pale lamplight, we could just see a stone fireplace facing us, with a mantelpiece from which hung a red valance - with bobbles. A sad fire smoked non-stop, but through the smoke we could still see the text: 'Thou, God, see-est me.' above the mantelpiece. There was the chairs and the table, and the fox in a glass case, and the iron bed with the patchwork quilt on it behind a curtain hanging across the corner.

"That's my bedroom," said Siencyn. "The floor's not very even yet, but it'll come." He had put bricks under two of the legs of the bed, but I felt he'd have to hold on tight so as not to roll out of bed when he tried to go to sleep.

"It's lovely," I said.

Siencyn beamed at me. "You're a very clever little gel - go far you will. This is all her idea, you know," he added. Mam looked at me, and the Policeman didn't seem very pleased with me neither.

"It's History," I told them. "It's all in History lessons."

"Well," said the Policeman. "A man can't be put in prison for taking his own furniture - it's all here, I suppose, all that's on my list of missing articles."

Oddjobs chuckled. "Was Marged mad? Oh, I'd have give a hundred pound to see her face when she saw what I did. But I'm not going back no more, no not never. She sold my chickens, so I'm not going back to that old miseryguts no more."

"Shame on you," said Mam. "Upsetting a good woman like that."

"I'm sick of good women," said Oddjobs. "And all that polishing and dusting, and banging mats about. Here I can do what I like, and if I want to spit in the fire, I'll spit in the fire, and no Marged to stop me!"

"Well, that's your affair," said the Policeman. "But trespassing's another thing. You are on Meredith Jones' land, in his old shed, so out you get."

"It's not an old shed," said Siencyn, all indignant. "If you see it in the light you'll see I've made it a proper house. Glass in the windows and all. Anyway, Meredith Jones saw me doing all this work, and he said it's all right by him, so there."

"There's no sanitation," said the Policeman.

"There's a stand-by tap in the quarry, and tomorrow I'm starting to build myself a lovely lav."

"Time to go," said Mam firmly. We all left, the Policeman saying something about his sergeant dealing with things, and Mam cross with everybody, and Dadda grinning all over his face.

"Goodnight," I called, as once more I jogged off on the Policeman's back. "It's a lovely, lovely house, Mr Siencyns!"

We went back the way we had come, through the soft, damp night. An owl hooted, and there was rustling in the long grass. Soon we were back outside Marged's house. The Policeman put me down. The rain had stopped.

"No more mud round here," he said. "Well, I better go in and tell Mrs Siencyn what's happened. *Darro*, there's going to be a row."

He walked up the path to give the good news that Siencyn was safe, but he didn't look as if he was expecting much of a welcome.

Me and Mam and Dadda walked home. Although I had never been up so late in my life, I wasn't sleepy. We walked in silence. When we got in, Mam lit the gas, and suddenly turned to me.

"Megan," she said. "I want you to promise me faithful that in all your life you'll never tell Siencyn Oddjobs no more History. Do you hear me? No more History."

"I promise," I said, although I couldn't see why.

"Off to bed," said Mam. "I'll be up in a minute."

"Goodnight," I said, kissed Dadda, and slowly climbed the stairs. I stopped. Mam and Dadda was talking, and Dadda was laughing. I could hear Mam's voice clearly.

"I don't care what you say. History is all very well, but just let Siencyn Oddjobs get a whiff about the French Revolution, and he'd have the colliery manager and the overmen on his cart, and he'd be handing out free knitting wool to all the women in the auction."

As I fell asleep, I felt I had the responsibility for the safety of all those men in my hands! It was very worrying, still, perhaps tomorrow I'd look up the Encyclopaedia and see what the French Revolution was all about.

CHAPTER 2

THE HARVEST FESTIVAL

I ran home from school one day, bursting with excitement. I had nine out of ten, and Miss Thomas said it was very good. We had to write all about a room, or a house, or a chapel or a church; anything we liked, and remember all the things we'd seen inside it. Mary Rees wrote about her Aunty in Cardiff's house, but she only got six out of ten.

Mam was making toast for tea, while my Aunty Scissors Ann was laying the table. Her real name was Cissie Ann, but I got it wrong when I was little and never got round to putting it right. Anyway she was sharp as scissors, so it suited her. Mam put another piece of bread on to the toasting fork, and held it to the fire.

"There's a good girl," she said. "Well done. What did you write about then?"

"Well," I said, then stopped. I had written all about Siencyn Oddjobs' shack up past the quarry - about his earthen floor, and rickety bed, and the chickens he kept in a cwtch made of old tea chests, but which kept getting out and perching on the back of his chairs or pecking for food on the table!

The trouble was that Mam didn't know that me and Dadda used to go and see old Oddjobs. It wasn't that we told a lie - we never said we didn't ever go to see him, it was just that we never got round to telling her that we did.

She couldn't abide Siencyn Oddjobs, especially since he left his wife. She said that *that* way of carrying on might be all right in some places - Hollywood or London or Cardiff - but not here. He only got his new chickens too, to spite Mrs Oddjobs, so all the women in the place sided with her, while all the men had a weak spot for him.

I thought I had better talk about something else.

"And we're going to have Harvest Festival in school on Friday," I said. "We've got to take fruit or vegetables and we're going to put them in the Hall and sing Hymns about the Harvest, and then the teachers and the Governess are going to give them to the Poor and Needy on Saturday. Can I take something nice?"

Aunty Scissors Ann sniffed. "You could call most of the children in your class Poor and Needy. Poor dabs, half of them haven't got shoes to their feet. How can they afford to take fruit and such like to this Harvest Festival carryon?"

"Mrs Thomas said if you haven't got any fruit to take, you can take fruits of the hedgerows. They're free. You can take Blackberries or berries from the bara caws tree, or wild flowers. But I can take something nice, can't I Mam? Please, Mam, can't I?"

Mam buttered the toast. "Come and have your tea, *merch i*. Well now what would you like to take to school? A nice apple or an orange?"

I bit into hot toast and the melted butter dribbled down my chin. "I don't know Mam. Mary Rees said she's taking grapes."

"Grapes!" Aunty Scissors Ann gave another sniff. "This isn't Buckingham Palace. Who can afford grapes, I'd like to know?"

"If I was Poor and Needy I'd like grapes," I said. "If I was a Poor and Needy I'd like a peach."

"Peaches now, is it?" scorned Aunty Scissors Ann "Hoity, Toity."

"Why shouldn't poor people have a nice treat now and then?" said Mam. "It isn't only rich people enjoy nice food - it's just that poor people don't get much chance to get used to it. I tell you what - I'll get something for you for Friday - it'll be a surprise - don't ask any questions. Leave it all to me."

"Oh thank you Mam," I said. But Aunty Scissors Ann said, "You spoil that child," and took some more toast. I didn't like Aunty Scissors Ann.

I was excited when I went home from school dinner time on Friday. We'd done nothing but talk about the Harvest Festival for days, and we'd been practising the Harvest Hymns and songs: 'All Things Bright and Beautiful,' and 'We Plough the Fields and Scatter.' I always used to wonder why we scattered after we'd ploughed the fields. Didn't the farmer want us to do it? Was he angry with us, and chased us, so we had to scatter from him? I often felt I couldn't understand Hymns.

"Is my Harvest Festival ready, Mam?" I asked.

"Come you and see," said Mam. We went into the parlour, and there it was.

"Oh Mam," I said. "It's the most wonderful Harvest in the world! It'll be the best anybody will bring."

Mam had got a cardboard box from Thomas and Evans, and had covered it with green crepe paper, with a big paper bow on the front. In the box she had put four apples, four oranges, some tomatoes, two bananas and in the middle, on a white paper doyley, a beautiful pink and gold peach, with some grapes each side of it. We'd never had so much fruit at one time in the house before.

"It must have cost ever so much," I said, but Mam said, "I hope some poor dab will really enjoy all this. It's not often I get to feel that I've done something special. I'm glad I spent the money - never mind what your Aunty says."

I couldn't eat my dinner - although it was sprats - I felt so proud!

At last it was time to go, and the box was so heavy Mam had to help me carry it to school. Everybody seemed to be bringing something - the school playground was full of lovely colours. Mam watched us marching into school, and waved 'Goodbye' smiling and looking pleased.

After Miss Thomas marked the register, we marched into the Hall while Miss Jones played the piano, and then we sang 'Come, Ye Thankful People, Come,' and afterwards put our Harvest on to the Big Table on the Governess' platform. It all looked so beautiful - Michaelmas Daisies, and Dahlias, and the fruits of the orchard, and the fruits of the hedgerows, and the fruits of the greengrocers. I loved it all, and in the middle of all this richness, was my special Harvest.

The next day was Saturday. Dadda was working the six-to-two shift, so after he'd had his bath, and his dinner, we went for a walk while Mam went to Ponty Market. It was a lovely afternoon, all sunshine and blue sky, with the bracken already turning red and the trees yellow and gold. We walked up along the top of the mountain, and looked down on our valley, and the houses and the people, and even the pit itself, looked like toys.

"Let's call in and see how Siencyn Oddjobs is, Dadda," I said, and he said, "Righto," so we climbed down through the brambles with the big blackberries, till we came to the shack.

Siencyn was sitting on a stool outside his door, smoking his black pipe, and enjoying the sunshine. When he saw us, he said, "Come you in - the kettle's on the boil! I was just going to wet the tea!" He went in and we followed.

"Never mind the tea for a minute," said Dadda (the cups was always a bit grubby). "Just let us sit for a spell. We've been all along from Hafod Ganol to Coed y Brenin, it's a tidy step and Megan's a little bit tired."

Oddjobs shoo'd a chicken off a chair, and told me to sit on it. "Them chickens will be laying soon," he said. "I'll make money out of them yet!"

I liked it in the shack. I liked the way Dadda and Oddjobs smoked their pipes, and talked, and forgot I was there. Although the smoke and dust was thick, there was a comfort about the place. Dadda and Oddjobs talked on, and I listened, until suddenly, there was a knock on the door.

"*Diawch*," said Oddjobs. "Who's that? I don't get no callers to come knocking." He went to the door and opened it. There on the doorstep, was our Governess, and my teacher Miss Thomas! We stared at them, and they stared at us.

"Good afternoon. May we come in?" asked Miss Thomas.

"Ay, ay come you in," said Oddjobs.

"Thank you," said the Governess.

They came in, and then I realised what they were carrying - my Harvest Festival! Miss Evans went on. "We have brought you this gift, from the children of the Junior School in order to give thanks for all the gifts from our Bountiful Creator. The children brought gifts of produce to be distributed to all those poor and needy who would benefit from them. We hope you enjoy this magnificent box of fruit. Where shall we put it?"

She looked around - the table was covered with newspaper for a cloth, and the remains of Oddjobs' breakfast and Dinner, and a bucket of chickens' mash.

Oddjobs put the bucket on the floor and said, "Put it by there miss, on the table." Miss Thomas did so, and Oddjobs cleared his throat several times, and then said, "Well Miss, and you too Miss, thank you for the fruit. Beautiful it is - beautiful. Aye, thank you indeed!" He looked around helplessly, and then said, "Like a cup of tea, now you're here?"

Miss Evans and Miss Thomas both said, "No thank you," so quickly, you'd have thought the words came out of one mouth. "We must go," said Miss Evans. "We have many more gifts to distribute. This one, I might tell you, is the best we have." Turning to me, she put her hand on my shoulder, and added, "I must tell you that your name, Mr Jenkins, heads the list of those receiving gifts because of a Composition written by this dear child. She described your sad conditions so accurately." She looked round at the broken window pane, stuffed with old socks, the red velvet valance with bobbles already sooty and singed, the rag rug with a big burn in the middle. She sighed, and shook her head sadly. "A really accurate description. Poor man. Good afternoon and Good afternoon to you Mr Williams. Megan is doing very well in school." She patted my shoulder, and the two ladies left, shaking their heads and tut-tutting.

Siencyn Oddjobs shut his door, and came in. Lifting his cap, he scratched his head and said, "What the elephant was all that? I couldn't understand what they was on about."

"Never mind what it was all about," said Dadda. "Just you get your teeth into that lot."

"Teeth! I can't eat them apples!" said Siencyn. "My teeth is gone, but them tomatoes would be nice with a bit of cheese for my supper, and I can manage the bananas, but what the 'eck do I want all this fruit for? Look, you have some of it. Take you the apples and let Megan *fach* have the peach, isn't it?"

I looked at Dadda. "Go on," he said. "Pity to waste it." So we shared the fruit between us. As I bit the peach the juice spurted out, Dadda quickly tied his hankie around my neck. "Don't get any mess on your cardigan," he said. "Mam would only ask how it got there!" I ate the grapes, and Dadda ate two apples, and he put the other two in his pocket, for after, and then we had a big orange between us.

"Here you are," said Siencyn. "You can have this nice box with the crinkly paper, to make a bed for your doll."

"No thanks," said Dadda. "She have got a doll's cot." To me, he whispered, "Better not, isn't it?"

I agreed. "Better not because of Mam."

We went home soon after that, leaving Oddjobs toasting the tomatoes and a bit of cheese on a plate in front of the fire.

As soon as we got away from the shack, Dadda said, "I don't think I'd mention any of this to Mam when we get home!"

"All right," I said, so we didn't. We told Mam we'd had a lovely walk, and she told us about the market and all the people she'd met, and what she'd bought, and the time went quickly until it was time to go to bed. When I kissed Dadda 'Goodnight', he winked at me.

Mam came with me upstairs. In my bedroom it was nearly as light as day - "It's the Harvest moon," said Mam. "Isn't it beautiful? So rich and round and silver as a sixpence."

She listened to my prayers and tucked me up, and kissed me 'Goodnight'.

Just as she was leaving the bedroom, she stopped, and said, "I wonder what Poor and Needy person had your Harvest Offering. I don't suppose we'll ever know. Still, I hopes as how they enjoyed it. They deserve to. It's good to have a treat now and then. Night, night, *cariad*."

As I settled myself to sleep, I felt I could still taste the peach and the grapes. It was sometimes rather nice to be one of the Poor and Needy, as long as Mam didn't know!

CHAPTER 3

DUCKING APPLE NIGHT

"Ducking Apple Night Tuesday," said Mam. "And Mrs Powell's asked us to go over there because Dadda's working days. I'll make a bit of Taffy to take with us, because they got enough apples. We'll go over after tea and be back in plenty of time to put Dadda's supper in the oven and boil the water for his bath. I can leave the bucket on the hob to warm up before we go."

"Oh Mam," I said. "There's lovely."

Sometimes life was so wonderful, I felt as if I was flying inside. I couldn't wait till Tuesday came; I was all excited and jumpy.

It rained on Tuesday, but that didn't matter - it wasn't like Bonfire Night. When we got to Mrs Powell's house there were about six other children there, and Mr Powell had tied apples on long strings and hung them from the wire clothes line that hung from hooks all around the room. There was some other mothers there too, and we had great fun, trying to take a bite out of the apples as they swung about. Mary Rees tried to cheat by holding the apple with her hand, and Billy Phillips punched her, and she cried, and Billy's mother smacked him. So then we did the ducking apples instead. Mrs Powell filled the small bath with water, and put it on the floor, and put some apples in it. They floated and bobbled about, and we took turns to try and pick up the apples with our teeth. Mr Powell was ever so funny; he took his teeth out and tried to get the apples out with no teeth.

We laughed and laughed.

Then Mrs Powell said she'd make a cup in hand for the grown-ups, and we had to take our taffy in to Mary Powell's grandmother, who lived in the front room. She was a round little lady, with small glasses on her nose, and a long skirt and striped flannel apron. Her shawl was fastened with a brooch that had MIZPAH on it. I thought I'd like to have a brooch with my name on it, like that. Old Mrs Powell had the gas turned down low because she said it was best for her eyes, but there was a lovely fire in the grate, and the room was nice and warm. We all sat on her bed. The brass bedstead twinkled and shone in the firelight and showed up the pretty patterns in her patchwork quilt. She took a piece of taffy, for after we'd gone, and we all sucked and chewed at ours.

"Tell us a story, Mamgu," said Mary Powell.

"You don't want any of my old stories," said her Grandmother. She was sitting by the fire in a rocking chair with a red plush cloth on it, and she had her feet on the fender, nice and comfy.

"Come on Mamgu. Please," said Mary Powell, so the old lady laughed and told us about the time when she'd been a servant on a big farm down in the Vale, and they'd had good times at haymaking and harvest and going to the Fair. I enjoyed that ever so much, but then she said, "I don't know if I ought to tell you this."

"Go on," we all said. This sounded exciting - something we weren't supposed to hear! "Well," she went on. "We had a man on our farm called Old Joe, and one day, we couldn't find him nowhere. Farmer thought he'd run off somewhere - not coming in for breakfast, or getting on with the swedes. Well, we was all sitting round the table in the big kitchen having our supper, all the men on the farm and us girls, when the Missus looks up and she screams. And we all looks up and there's blood coming through the ceiling on to the table cloth. It was Old Joe's blood! A murderer had killed him and put his body up in the room we stored the apples in. The blood was coming all over the place - dripping and dripping and dripping!"

I was so frightened my stomach hurt and the world went black. To think a murderer could kill people! To think murderers could go about the place and no-one stopped them, and the blood was everywhere. I wondered if the murderers had come to our street. Perhaps one was already hiding in our house until we came home, and Dadda wouldn't be there till after ten o'clock and we could be dead by then. I was too afraid to cry, and when Mam came for me, I was scared to go out into the black night.

When we got home, the house was dark, except for the firelight in the kitchen. The flames made shadows move and dart about the room - I wondered if one of them was the murderer's shadow. Mam lit the gas, and made my cocoa for supper, but when she said it was time for bed, I cried and wouldn't go because I was afraid to go upstairs.

"What's the matter?" asked Mam. "You've never been like this before."

At first I was crying too much to tell her, but at last I blurted out that it was the murderer who was frightening me.

"What murderer?" asked Mam, so I told her. She was very cross with Old Mrs Powell - "Her and her old stories," she said. "Not a grain of truth in them. Senile she is. Don't you go taking no notice of her."

The harm was done, though, and I was afraid to go to bed for a long time after that. I had to have a night light, and Mam had to sit by me till I went to sleep.

The autumn became winter. Aunty Scissors Ann went to stay with her sister in Swansea who fell and broke her leg, and my cousin Billy had dinner with us every day. He'd lost his job as errand boy for Pugh's Grocer because he was grown too big for the shop bike. I was glad Billy was around. He said he'd make sure no murderer got me.

Then it was time for Aunty Scissors Ann to come home. Mam went to her house to dust and clean, and see the fire was all right, and put a bit of dinner on. I went with her, and me and Billy played Snakes and Ladders. Suddenly the front door slammed and Aunty Scissors Ann was home. She came rushing into the kitchen where Mam was laying the table.

"Hello," said Mam. "Caught the early bus, did you?"

"Yes," snapped Aunty Scissors Ann. "I caught the early bus all right. But that's not the only thing I caught. Here's me going off to do a kindness, and hard work it was with two fires a day, and washing; but my only son goes and shames me behind my back!"

"Shamed you!" said Mam. "How have Billy shamed you? He couldn't help it if Pugh Grocer sacked him because he was too mean to put him on the bacon counter and train him proper in the grocery line."

"I'm not talking about that. I'm talking about undesirable characters sneaking into this house behind my back when I was gone." Aunty Scissors Ann banged her bag on the table and looked daggers at us. "Soon as I get off the bus Millie Evans told me she'd seen Siencyn Oddjobs creeping into my home the back lane way so that no one would see him."

"Not very successful was he, if Millie Evans had her beady eyes on him?" said Billy.

"Carrying something in a bag he was," went on Aunty Scissors Ann. "Something secret, she said. There's a nice thing, isn't it? Me in Swansea, and Siencyn Oddjobs lording it by here. To think that I would live to see the day that foxy old flag should have crossed my doorstep. Him and his nasty sneaky ways. Oh! The shame of it."

"What's wrong with Siencyn Oddjobs coming round here to keep me company a bit?" said Billy. "I'm on the dole, and there's all day to do nothing! My butties lucky enough to be down the pit, and me with no chance of a job, and no money to do nothing with."

"You're not having that Siencyn Oddjobs in my house ever again, and I'm not having no argument." Aunty Scissors Ann was really getting her moss off by now.

"It's my home as well," shouted Billy. "You're always on to me. Just because old Siencyn came round here a bit, you carry on as if I'm a criminal. No feeling for me now I've lost my job, just nag, nag, nag, all the time. It's enough to drive anybody out of their mind. I'm sick and fed up with it all." And Billy suddenly pushed past Aunty Scissors Ann and ran upstairs and slammed his bedroom door.

"Well," said Aunty Scissors Ann. "If I should live to see the day my flesh and blood talked back to me like that."

"Serves you right," said Mam. "You shouldn't have spoke to him like that. The poor boy breaking his heart over the way Pugh Grocer treated him, and you, his own mother, going on so unsympathetic. Here, sit down and have a cup of tea and stop acting like a bear with a sore head."

Aunty Scissors Ann flopped into the chair by the fire and began to cry. She sniffed into her hankie and wiped her eyes and blew her nose.

"If I'm judged in heaven as I'm judged here," she began.

"Drink your tea," said Mam, putting two spoons of sugar in her cup. Aunty began to drink her tea, and sniff, and sip. Mam gave me some tea, and some biscuits. I dipped them in my tea, and enjoyed them.

"You spoil that child," said Aunty Scissors Ann, about me.

Suddenly there was a terrible noise, a loud bang like a sharp crack of thunder, from upstairs. Aunty Scissors Ann screamed and tipped her tea over her lap. Mam dropped the milk jug and it smashed her cup.

"*Cato'n pawb*," she cried. "What's that?"

The noise came from over my head. I looked up. Suddenly I started screaming. In the corner of the ceiling a red stain appeared - it began to spread and spread.

"He's killed him!" I screamed. "He's killed him!"

Mam and Aunty Scissors Ann looked up. Aunty Scissors Ann screamed, "He's shot hisself!" she yelled. "Billy's shot hisself. I drove him to it. Drove him to it I did."

"Stay by here," ordered Mam. "I'm going to see."

"No," I cried. "Don't go Mam," but already Mam was going out of the kitchen, and up the stairs. I heard her footsteps as she rushed along the landing, then there was voices - Mam's and a man's.

'She's talking to the murderer, I thought. 'The murderer's come for us all.' But Aunty Scissors Ann jumped up, crying, "It's my Billy's voice!" And she was off upstairs like a shot. I ran after her.

The back bedroom door was open, and Mam and Billy were there. A pool of red was on the floor and smashed glass everywhere. 'The blood...' I thought.

"I told the old flag not to put the corks too tight too soon," Billy was saying.

"Oh, my lovely boy," cried Aunty Scissors Ann, holding on to Billy. "Oh, thank heaven you're all right."

"What is it?" Mam said. "Elderberry?"

"Aye," said Billy. "I never made wine before, but Siencyn Oddjobs said he'd done it hundreds of times. He got bottles from I don't know where, and we got the elderberries from down by the river. I made some beetroot wine as well. Thought we'd have a bit of wine at Christmas to cheer us up like, and I could give some for presents. Fat lot I'll be able to give this year, with money so tight. I got a book out of the library as well, just to make sure what we had to do. I can't seem to do nothing right these days!"

"Never you mind," said Aunty Scissors Ann. "I'll clean this old mess up in no time, and if you want to make some more wine, I'll give you a hand. Made it for my Mam I used to, and I still remember what to do."

"Strong drink is raging," I said, remembering the Band of Hope.

"Not much raging about elderberry or beetroot," said Aunty Scissors Ann, still holding on to Billy, as if she'd eat him.

"Come on Megan," said Mam. "Time to go. See you in Chapel tomorrow, you two." And she got me downstairs and into my coat and off down the street before you could say 'Jack Robinson'."

She told Dadda all about it, when he came home. He sat on his stool in front of the fire, taking off his pit clothes and putting them in his box. Mam filled the bath with water from the bucket on the hob.

"Well," he said. "If that don't beat all! Make Cissie Ann treat Billy decent now, that fright will. You got to agree, Siencyn Oddjobs did a good turn there. What do it say in the Bible about 'Peace Makers', Megan?"

"It do say, 'Blessed are the Peace Makers, because they shall be called the children of God'," I told him.

"Well then, it's 'Blessed be Siencyn Oddjobs, for he have done the impossible' - made Cissie Ann human for five minutes, and got peace between her and Billy." Dadda lathered the flannel, and Mam began to wash his back.

"Will Siencyn grow a halo?" I asked.

"Sure to," said Dadda, and he laughed and laughed.

CHAPTER 4

A 'NATTENDANT' ELF

"You've heard the latest, I suppose," said Aunty Scissors Ann. She had just happened to be passing and called in to see what we was doing. "Sunday School Christmas Party three weeks today, and they're going to have a Father Christmas! Ruining the children with all this nonsense - teach them to expect too much it will."

"What's wrong with Father Christmas at Christmas time?" asked Dadda, who was mending my doll's cot on the kitchen table. "Now if you had Father Christmas on St David's Day, that'd be a bit unusual like!"

"You know very well what I mean," sniffed Aunty Scissors Ann. "Every year it's the same. Give out the date of the Sunday School Party, and children from all over the shop turn up on Sundays regular as clockwork. As soon as the party's over, they stop coming till it's time for the outing to Barry Island in the summer. I know their ways!"

"At least they come," said Mam. "A little seed of faith could very well be planted in that short time."

"Never," snapped Aunty Scissors Ann. "Making a convenience of the Chapel, that's what they're doing. And if they find out there's going to be a Father Christmas, it wouldn't surprise me if they came from other Sunday Schools too. Accused of poaching that's what we'll be!"

"No-one's to know about Father Christmas," said Mam. "It's a closely guarded secret." .

"Megan do know! Look at her listening," said Aunty Scissors Ann. "She'll tell all her friends in school, and it'll be all over the auction in no time."

"Megan can keep a secret better than some people I know," said Mam. "Anyway you don't have to help if you don't want to. "Gwyn, get that mess off the table, I want to lay tea."

"I've finished," said Dadda. "Here, *merch i*, good as new. Cost you a kiss, it will."

As I kissed and hugged my father, Aunty Scissors Ann snapped, "You spoil that child," and she opened the back door with a bad tempered click, and closed it behind her with a slam that shook the dishes on the dresser.

"Not much spirit of Christmas about Cissie Ann," said Dadda, starting to put his tools away. "I wonder what she'd say if she knew I was going to be Father Christmas!"

"She'd have a fit," said Mam.

It was nice being in the secret. I'd seen Dadda trying on his outfit. He looked lovely in it.

There was red trousers and coat with a black shiny belt, and a red hat with cotton wool round it, and he was going to wear his wellingtons. When he put the beard on, and stuck them eyebrows on with special glue, you'd never know who it was. The best part of the secret was that Mr Watkins, the Sunday School Superintendent, decided it would be a good idea if Father Christmas had a Natendant Elf, and to keep it in the family - I was it!

Mam made me a lovely outfit of red baggy knickers stuffed with cotton wool, a top with Zig-Zags round it, and a cap with great big pointy ears - they were stuffed with cotton wool too, and I had cotton wool whiskers, so no-one would know who I was. Mam used a whole roll of cotton wool on the outfit!

Mr Watkins came and told Dadda and me what to do at the party. We had to go into the kitchen the back way. Mr Jones the Fish would have some bells on a stick, and he would shake them, and then we would go into the vestry. The children would line up and I would hand Father Christmas a parcel - blue wrapping paper for a boy, and pink wrapping paper if it was a girl. Then, when we'd given out the presents, we could wave to everybody, go back into the kitchen, and Mr Jones the Fish would shake the bells again, then we had to go quickly away before anybody saw us. Mr Watkins wanted Dadda to say "Happy Christmas Children," and ask them if they'd all been good, but Dadda said the fluff from his whiskers got down his mouth if he opened it, so it was decided Mr Watkins would do all the talking instead.

As the day came nearer, I got more and more excited, and Mam doubled my dose of cod liver oil and malt every morning to keep my strength up.

At last the party day arrived, and Mam went over the arrangements again for the umpteenth time.

"You dress by here, and don't forget Megan keeps her black stockings on. See Megan's coat is buttoned up to the chin before you leave the house. She needn't wear a hat, because the cotton wool ears will be warm enough, but she must wear her coat and scarf - and gloves too. Now then, it takes ten minutes to walk from here to the Chapel vestry (Mam had timed it with our alarm clock), you are expected to arrive at quarter to five. By then the tea and the games will be over, so leave here at twenty-five to five on the dot. Alright?"

"Alright, sergeant major," said Dadda, saluting like a soldier in the pictures. "You've told me enough times. I know what to do. What could go wrong?"

"I don't know," said Mam. "But I've got a funny feeling in my bones."

She put on her coat and hat and just as she was sticking the hat pins in, the latch on the back door clicked and in comes Aunty Scissors Ann.

"You ready?" she asked Mam.

"Oh ho!" said Dadda. "Thought you didn't think much of Sunday School Parties. Changed your mind, have you?"

"I know my duty," said Aunty Scissors Ann, her lips pursed like a prune. "If my Chapel needs my help, I'm more than ready and willing to give it. I'm the one in charge of the helper's teas. Come on Bethan if we don't get off we'll never get the water boiled. That boiler is real awkward. Takes hours to get going it do, even if the wind is in the right direction and the coal is best anthracite. Come on."

"I'm ready," said Mam, looking worried as if she was going to the dentists. "Now, don't forget, twenty-five to five. So long." and they were off, and the front door knocker tap - tap - tapping as they shut the door tight.

"Go anywhere for a free meal would Aunty Cissie Ann," said Dadda. "She can smell a free ham sandwich a mile away."

We had a game of Ludo and had the tea Mam had left for us, and wished time would go more quickly. The hands of the clock seemed to be stuck all the time. At last, Dadda said, "Right, time for you to dress." So I put my puffy knickers on over my black stockings, and my red top with the Zig-Zags, and I was just doing up the belt when we heard a tap at the kitchen window. We looked up. There was Siencyn Oddjobs peering at us over the net curtain.

"Now what does the old flag want?" asked Dadda, as he opened the back door. "What's the matter? Come you in. You only just caught me - I'm off to be Father Christmas at the Sunday School Party."

"Good job I caught you then," said Siencyn. "I saw Mrs Williams and Cissie Ann going off earlier, so I knew you'd be on you own, like. I'm doing a job for Silas Soames - his coal cwtch roof is leaking, but I've run out of tile nails. Only want a couple I do, and I wondered if you could let me have a lend of a handful?"

"I don't think so," said Dadda. "And I haven't got time to go up to the shed to look. There might be some in my box of bits in the cwtch under the stairs. Come you near the fire, and I'll have a look."

Siencyn put his bag of tools on the floor, and stood by the fire warming his hands.

"It's bitter out," he said. "And getting foggy. I wouldn't be surprised if we had snow for Christmas."

"Here we are," said Dadda. He shut the door of the cwtch behind him and rummaged in the old biscuit tin where he kept odd nails and screws and bits of string. "Here's two and here's another one." He moved the clinking metal pieces around with his finger as he walked. "Looks as if that's the lot." And with that, he fell smack over Siencyn's bag of tools. There was a thump as he hit his head on the table, and a bump as he hit the floor!

"Oh *Darro*!" said Siencyn. "You all right Mr Williams?"

"No, I'm not," groaned Dadda, trying to pull himself up on to a chair. "It's my ankle. I can't put my weight on it."

'Oh no!' I thought. 'Nearly time to go and Dadda in agony.' We put a wet towel on his ankle, which was all swelled up, and Mam's wet dish cloth on the bump on his forehead, which was coming up like a shiny red egg.

"I'll get the doctor," said Siencyn.

"Don't be daft," said Dadda. "Nothing broke, look - I can wiggle my toes. Sprained it I have, real bad too, but there's no need for no doctor. I can't get to the Christmas Party though, that's for sure. You and your blinking tile nails. We can't disappoint them children. What can we do? You'll have to go instead of me!"

"Me!" said Siencyn. "Me be Father Christmas!" Suddenly he grinned. "Me be Father Christmas in the Sunday School Party! If that don't beat all. What have I got to do?"

"Megan will tell you," said Dadda. "Just get into the Father Christmas outfit and look sharp."

The trouble was, Siencyn was thinner than Dadda, and shorter too. When he put the red trousers on, they wouldn't stay up.

"Stuff him with cushions back and front," said Dadda. "Go you into the front room, Megan, and fetch them from the sofa."

"But they're Mam's best cushions!" I said. "What will Mam say?"

"Desperate remedies, *cariad*," said Dadda, so I fetched the cushions and Siencyn stuffed them down the trousers back and front, but by the time he'd got the red coat on the cushions had fell down in his trousers and made big lumps around his knees.

"Safety pins," cried Dadda. "Where do Mam keep her safety pins?"

"In her work box," I said. "And there's some in the Coronation mug on the mantelpiece. I'll get them."

Dadda tried to pin the cushions to Siencyn's jacket, back and front, but it wasn't easy, because he had his bad leg on a stool in front of his chair, and every time he moved he shouted "Owww!" Siencyn pulled the trousers up over the cushions and this time they stayed up. He did up the big buttons on the front of the Father Christmas coat, and put on the hat and the whiskers and I stuck his eyebrows on with the special glue. They were a bit lopsided, but they had to do.

"Right," said Dadda. "You look champion. Now, Megan, put your whiskers on, and your elf hat and then wrap up warm like Mam said, and for goodness sake get going!"

"Will you be all right Dadda?" I asked. "Shall I tell Mam?"

"No, No, not till she comes back! Or she'll come tearing home and put me in splints. I'll be fine. Just leave me be."

We weren't all that late leaving the house. It was very cold outside, and the fog made misty rings round the street lamps. We was nearly by the Chapel vestry when Siencyn said suddenly, "Thirsty I'll be, being Father Christmas. You wait by here while I pop in this shop for a drink of lemonade," and like a rabbit down a hole, he disappeared into the Red Cow.

It was cold and rather frightening being all by myself outside the Public House - shop indeed! 'I'm not daft,' I told myself, although I knew Mam would be tamping if she could see me waiting outside this particular 'Sink of Iniquity'. The swing doors opened and a man came out. He held on to the door posts, and swayed a bit. "Nowell, nowell," he sang, then he saw me. His eyes opened wide. I stood under the misty gas lamps - a short, fat figure with a pointed head and pointed ears.

"I need another drink," he said, as he fell back inside.

Two minutes later the doors opened again and I heard loud, gruff laughter and Siencyn came out with a large sprig of Mistletoe in his cap.

"That's better," he said. "Come on, *fach*, let's put a move on."

Soon the lights of the Chapel vestry glowed pale in the fog. We went round to the back of the Chapel past the gravestones and it was a relief when Siencyn opened the door and we saw the lights in the kitchen and heard the clinking of crockery and the sound of the ladies chatting as they started on the washing up. Clouds of steam was coming out of the boiler, and Aunty Scissors Ann was ladling hot water into the stone sink.

"Here they are," said Mam. "This old fog haven't got down your chest, Megan, have it?"

"No," I said.

"Don't talk, either of you, you'll get bits of your whiskers in your mouth."

"Leave the washing up, ladies," called the minister's wife. "Go you and sit out the front with the children, to enjoy the fun. I'll tell Mr Watkins you're here. Here's the sack of presents."

She rounded up the lady helpers like a fussy sheepdog. Through the half open kitchen door, we could see them making their way into the brightly lit vestry and sitting in a row by the Christmas Tree. The noise in the vestry was lovely, all laughing and excited, then Mr Watkins rang his bell and there was silence. We could hear the steady hiss of the gas lamps.

Mr Jones the Fish quietly sidled into the kitchen, a stick with little bells on it in his hands.

"You look great, Gwyn," he said to Siencyn. "Wouldn't have guessed who you was if I didn't know!"

Siencyn nodded his head, and got behind me.

In the vestry, Mr Watkins was holding forth. "Now children, who brings presents at Christmas time?"

"Father Christmas!" chorused the assembled Sunday School.

"And does he bring them to naughty children, or to good children?"

"Good children," they shouted.

"And are you good children or naughty children?"

"Good children." The answer was yelled at the top of their lungs.

"Well, good children, be quiet and listen."

The silence was full of expectancy. Then Mr Jones the Fish shook his stick with the little bells, softly at first, then more loudly, then Mr Watkins opened the kitchen door wide and cried out, "Yes, it is! It's Father Christmas! And he's got an attendant Elf with him."

Siencyn picked up the sack of presents and we went into the crowded vestry. The children were sitting on benches all around the room and were gazing at us with big eyes and open mouths.

"Line up children, and Father Christmas will give you a present," said Mr Watkin. Some of the little ones begun to cry, but their mothers hushed them up.

Me and Siencyn stood in the middle of the room, and I took out the presents and he gave them to the children - blue for a boy, pink for a girl, just as Mam had said. As the children opened their presents they got all excited. They was lovely presents, dolls and little handbags and sewing sets and motor cars and lorries and books - not one costing less than 6d. It was real quality. At last we had finished. All the children had had a present. We walked back towards the Christmas tree, and the open kitchen door beyond.

"Three cheers for Father Christmas," called Mr Watkins.

The noise was deafening. We waved and turned to go.

Suddenly, Siencyn darted up to the bench where the ladies were sitting. Waving his mistletoe, he bent over Mam and gave her a smacking kiss - I heard it, even through his whiskers.

The children cheered again. Then he kissed Aunty Scissors Ann! More cheers! And then he kissed little Miss Williams, turned and waved, grabbed my hand and pulled me into the kitchen, where Mr Jones the Fish started to jingle the bells on a stick. There was so much excitement in the vestry, no-one could have heard Father Christmas's sleigh going up over the roofs and back to Iceland.

We hurried back through the graveyard and on to the road. This time Siencyn passed by the Red Cow without wanting any lemonade. Back through the ghostly fog we went and were soon home.

We had left the front door on the latch, so we went straight in.

"All right, Mr Williams?" asked Siencyn. "How you feeling now?"

"Still can't put my foot to the ground," said Dadda. "And my head thumps awful. How did you get on?"

"Fine," said Siencyn. "Real champion, went like clockwork. Megan *fach*, undo them safety pins, there's a good girl."

It didn't take long for him to get out of the Father Christmas outfit, and get his old mac and cloth cap and muffler back on. "Well, got to be going," he said. "I really enjoyed being Father Christmas. Mum's the word!

"Goodnight," he called as he waved through the back window. We heard the click of the back lane gate.

"He was in a hurry," said Dadda. "Still, perhaps it's all for the best. Mam wouldn't like it if she came back and found him here. Can't abide him, she can't, though I don't know why. No harm in old Siencyn."

I took my Nattendant Elf's costume off, and put my skirt and jumper back on.

"You got there in time then," said Dadda.

"Yes," I said. "We was only a little bit late - 'cos of Siencyn having a drink of lemonade in the Red Cow."

"He had WHAT?" asked Dadda.

"Lemonade," I said. "In the Red Cow."

"Oh no," groaned Dadda. "Oh, No!"

"He wasn't there long," I said. "And he was a good Father Christmas. He had mistletoe in his hat."

"What did he do with the mistletoe?" asked Dadda, sounding as if he expected the roof to fall in on him.

"He kissed Mam and Aunty Scissors Ann and little Miss Williams," I said. "In front of the whole Sunday School!"

"I'm sunk," moaned Dadda. "I'm real sunk. If Mam finds out she've been kissed by Siencyn Oddjobs you'll hear her shouting in Tonypandy. She'll kill me! She's bound to guess. I know her. Nothing gets past her."

He put his head in his hands, and then shouted, "Ow," as he hurt the lump on his head. I didn't know what to do. Suddenly he looked up and said, "Megan *fach*, go you into the pantry and fetch the bottle of tonic wine on the shelf by the chutney."

"But that's for Bopa Williams for Christmas," I said.

"Desperate remedies, *cariad*," said Dadda. "Real desperate." So I got the bottle and Dadda unscrewed the cork, and took big swallows of the tonic wine. Then he said, "Listen, here's Mam coming!" We could hear her saying 'Goodnight' to Aunty Scissors Ann by our front door. "Quick, pass me them cushions, and put them safety pins back in the mug."

When Mam came in, there was Dadda sitting in the armchair by the fire, his stocking feet on the best cushions on a stool, and he was leaning back with his eyes shut, and the dishcloth over his forehead.

"*Cato'n pawb!*" said Mam coming into the room and plonking her bag down on the table. "Whatever's the matter, Gwyn?"

"Dadda fell and hurt his ankle," I said.

"And my head," whispered Dadda, looking all sad and sorry for himself. "I'll be all right now just. Don't you worry."

"Where did you fall?" asked Mam.

"Dadda fell by there," I said. "By the cwtch under the stairs."

"There," said Mam. "I knew it. I knew that mat was getting frayed and I should have mended it. It's all my fault. Oh dear, that I should have let this happen. Let me see your head. Oh it's a real lump. Black and blue it'll be by the morning. I'll get a paper compress on it. Let me see the ankle."

"Nothing broke," said Dadda in his whispering voice. "Only a sprain."

"Sprains can be bad," said Mam. She leaned over to take the towel off his ankle and caught sight of the tonic wine on the shelf by the arm of his chair.

"Gwyn Williams," she said. "You've been imbibing! I wondered what possessed you to go mad with that mistletoe, and now I know. You had tonic wine to give you courage to be Father Christmas, and you went overboard with it. You must have drunk a good eggcup full! No wonder you fell down on that frayed mat. You are not used to strong drink, and this is the result. I thought I smelled alcohol on your breath when you kissed me in the vestry!"

"I feel awful," Dadda moaned.

"No wonder!" said Mam. "Never mind. I'll strap up your ankle, and put some of Grampa Wilkins' ointment on your head, and you'll be right as rain in the morning. Sit still now, I'll make you a nice cup of tea. Anything else you want. I've got some salmon sandwiches and ham left over from the party, and some slab cake too, if you fancy any."

"I think perhaps I'd better eat something," said Dadda. "Must keep my strength up."

So after Mam bandaged Dadda's head and strapped up his ankle, she made a pot of tea, and a cup of cocoa for me and we ate up all the party left overs.

"Now bed for you Megan," said Mam. My pyjamas was warming on the oven door. I went into the back kitchen to wash and clean my teeth. As I came back, I heard Mam saying to Dadda, "Fancy you kissing Cissie Ann! And little Miss Williams! She didn't half enjoy it. She was still all of a twitter when she went home! You'll have to have tonic wine more often, my lad. It's ages since you gave me a kiss like that! It made me go all hot and bothered, you Casanova, you." Humming happily to herself, she went upstairs to hang up her coat and hat.

Dadda's face went a sort of purpley red. Suddenly he said, "Casanova. I'll Casanova him! When I get hold of Siencyn Oddjobs, I'll Casanova him all the way to Tonypandy."

I didn't know what that meant, but by the look on Dadda's face, it must be something awful painful!

CHAPTER 5

THE CHRISTMAS TRUCE

"Christmas or no," said Mam. "I draw the line at having Siencyn Oddjobs here."

"No harm in old Siencyn," said Dadda. "Lonely he'll be at Christmas, all by hisself up in that old shack."

"Serve him right," said Mam, thumping the iron down on the trivet. She put the pillowcase on the pile that was ironed and picked up another one and started on that, "Leaving his poor wife all alone, and living in that pigsty up on the mountain. Why don't he go back to Marged instead of being a disgrace to us all. Down the Club every whip stich and drunk every Saturday regular! No he's not coming here for Christmas and that's flat. I've asked Cissie Ann and Billy, and Uncle Arthur and little Miss Williams to come to us on Christmas Day. And we'll go to Cissie Ann's Boxing Day."

Not much fun in that lot, I thought. Cousin Billy was all right. Working down the pit he was now, and happy as Larry, but Aunty Cissie Ann was always on at me. I didn't really like Aunty Cissie Ann.

Uncle Arthur wasn't really my Uncle neither. He lived with his sister who said she had to have one day off from looking after him, so she used to go to help serve dinners and wash up in the Workhouse on Christmas Day and we had Uncle Arthur. He was very quiet, but respectable.

Little Miss Williams was a dressmaker. She had a card in her front room window with 'E Williams, Dressmaker. Evening Gowns a Speciality' on it, but although she got orders for dresses and blouses and skirts, she never got any call for her speciality. The only one we knew who had a long frock was Madam Hepzibah Reese Jones LRAM Contralto, and hers had been to so many Celebrity Concerts, people used to say it could sing the 'Lost Chord' on its own. Little Miss Williams didn't have nobody to go to on Christmas Day so she came to us.

Before Christmas I saved up and bought presents for Mam and Dadda and hid them in my washstand. We made cards and calendars in school and paper chains and learnt new carols and sang old ones and I was an Angel of the Lord in the Nativity Play.

Mam made the pudding, and I had a stir and a wish, and we put a silver threepence in it, and then Mam made the cake and let me make the icing on it into snow by moving it round with a fork and we bought a Robin and a Father Christmas for it in Woolworths. It was lovely.

Then a few days before Christmas we had a letter from Auntie Bessie. I loved my Auntie Bessie. She was big and plump and wore pink knitted silk stretchy jumpers and had earrings as big as gob stoppers. She wore bright red lipstick and had her hair permed regular, and let me have her empty scent bottles to play with - Evening in Paris, Californian Poppy and a Devon Violet.

Cwtching up to Auntie Bessie was like burrowing into a warm bed. She was always laughing and eating sweets and chocolates, and she used to give me some. She was comfortably off. She had lots of Insurance money, because she had buried four husbands - in Swansea, Llanelli, Carmarthen and Porth, and she had a lovely time every year just before Flowering Sunday going round scrubbing their headstones and putting them tidy.

"Here's a letter from our Bessie," said Mam, when Dadda came home from the morning shift. "Says can she come for Christmas? Arriving Christmas Eve and she's joined the International League of Total Teetotallers. You never know what our Bessie is up to next. She's for ever trying something new. She's joined the Baptists and the Presbyterians and the Independents and the Missions to Seamen and now this lot - very strict TT they are - even don't allow Wine Gums! Mrs Rees Top House is a member, and Mrs Evans Vinegar Face. You'd think a woman as had lost four husbands would spend less time gallivanting and more time reflecting on life. Well, I'll write to say she can come and welcome. I'll go up and get the back bedroom ready."

"I'll help," I said. I was so excited that Auntie Bessie was coming - Christmas would be lovely with her staying with us.

We put the best sheets and pillowcases on the bed, and a blue counterpane - "Though why I put my bit of best for Bessie I don't know," said Mam. "Eat sweets in bed, she do. Last time after she'd gone back I found squashed chocolate under the pillow, and a sucked Minto stuck to the bottom sheet!"

We bought a Christmas tree in Ponty Market, and covered it with tinsel and lovely decoration that we'd had ever since I could remember. There was a silver bird with a long yellow tail, and a gold bell that tinkled when you walked pass the tree. We put trimmings up in the passage and the front room and the middle room, and Dadda laid the fires ready, because Christmas Day was the only day in the year we had a fire in all the rooms downstairs. We put Christmas cards on the mantelpieces and holly on the pictures and Dadda hung mistletoe up over the doors.

The house looked like a Palace.

Two days before Christmas Mog Price from the Lan Farm brought the goose. It was in a big basket, lying wrapped in a white muslin cloth, and a big bunch of sage was tucked under one of his wings. We put him in the cold pantry on the stone slab, and Aunty Scissors Ann and the neighbours came to have a look. They thought he was beautiful.

On Christmas Eve, Mam made mince pies, and a pie out of the goose giblets. I was making breadcrumbs for the stuffing, rubbing the stale bread round and round the colander with the back of my knuckles, when Auntie Bessie came.

"Give us a kiss, and put the kettle on," she called.

There's excitement! She hugged me and kissed me and gave me a bag of dolly mixtures, and said how lovely the house looked, and didn't the kitchen smell beautiful, with the mince pies and all, and she could do with a cup in hand if there was one going.

Mam put the kettle on and Dadda carried Auntie Bessie's case upstairs and I sat on her lap and felt that Christmas had come.

"Would you like me to show you my dolls after dinner?" I asked her, but she shook her head.

"I can't *cariad*," she said. "I've got to go out with the League and get people to join."

"But it's Christmas Eve," I objected.

"That's the best time," said Auntie Bessie. "Oh I'd give anything to get one TT of my very own. There might be someone out there ripe for signing the Pledge."

After dinner she was off to join the local League. "Strong drink is raging," she said as she buttoned her coat. "Don't expect me till late tonight. Where's my banner?"

I was disappointed, but still there was a lot to do. I watched as Mam stuffed the goose with sage and onions and my breadcrumbs and then I was allowed to stir the jelly till it melted and was poured into the mould. Dadda and me cleaned the sprouts ready, and we got out the best knives and forks, and the best plates that had belonged to Mamgu Jones, and soon the day had gone, and it was time for bed.

We hung up our stockings on the brass rail above the fire place in the kitchen. Mam lent one of hers to Auntie Bessie, and I wrote our names on pieces of paper, and safety pinned them on. I undressed by the fire, ran upstairs to my bed, which was warm from the hot brick wrapped in flannel that Mam had put there after tea.

'I'll never sleep,' I thought. 'I'm too excited,' but I must have gone off quite soon, and never heard Auntie Bessie coming home.

When I woke up there was the first glimmers of light in the dark sky.

'It's Christmas Day,' I thought, and ran in to Mam and Dad. "Wake up!" I shouted. "It's Christmas."

"It's early," said Dadda. "And freezing cold. You get into bed with Mam, and I'll go down and light the fire, and call you when it's warming up." He put his trousers and a pullover on over his pyjamas, and went down stairs. I cwtched up to Mam, all impatient to see my presents. It seems years before Dadda called, "Come you on down," and Mam put a shawl around my shoulders, and we called Auntie Bessie, and I ran down to see - Ooh! Such lovely things! The stockings bulging, and presents on the kitchen table - a doll that said "Mamma," and a little handbag, and puzzles and books, two new liberty bodices, (I knew where *they* came from), and sweets and a doll's tea set. Then the stocking, with a tangerine and an apple and nuts and a chocolate Father Christmas, and a new gold ha'penny right down in the toe. Dadda had coal and an old scrubbing brush in his stocking - how we laughed! Then Mam gave him a new shaving brush, and I gave him the shaving soap I'd bought. And scent for Mam, and a box of Pontifract cakes for Auntie Bessie, and we all admired my doll and looked at my books and had a wonderful time.

"Kettle on," said Mam. "And the goose in the oven."

As we had our breakfast, the warm kitchen was rich with the smell of the roasting goose. Dadda put a match to the fires in the parlour and the middle room. Auntie Bessie went off to join the League, because although the Pubs was shut the Clubs was open.

I played with my new toys, wearing my best dress, because it was Christmas.

How Mam worked! She performed miracles with the assortment of saucepans on the fire - the pudding boiling and the vegetables to cook and the custard and the gravy to stir so that there was no lumps. Then the table to lay in the Middle Room, best cloth and cruet and extra chairs brought down from upstairs, and where's the gravy boat? And is the goose done?

"Dinner at one o'clock," Mam had said, so Aunty Scissors Ann and Billy were there by twelve, and then Uncle Arthur came - empty handed - and little Miss Williams, with a box of crayons for me, and a bottle of Ginger Wine, and it is only once a year!

"No harm in Ginger Wine, and thank you," said Mam. "We'll all have a little drop after dinner."

Then the goose was put on the table, and the hot plates, and the vegetable dishes.

"Sit you all down," said Dadda, so we did, and he carved the goose and spooned out the stuffing, and I wondered where Auntie Bessie was.

Then just as the plates were piled high with sprouts and parsnips, and roast potatoes and mashed potatoes and slices of the goose and mounds of stuffing, here comes Auntie Bessie, standing in the doorway, pink and happy and excited.

"I've found one," she cried. "I've found someone to sign the Pledge. I've got a new member of my very own - found him outside the Non-Political Club before he could touch a drop, and I've brought him here with me!" She reached behind her and like a magician taking a rabbit out of a hat - she produced Siencyn Oddjobs! He stood there in his best Harris Tweed Suit and his strangling collar, grinning feebly.

There was a shocked silence, then Dadda said, "Sit you down and welcome! Billy, run upstairs to the front bedroom and fetch a chair, I'll get another plate!"

Mam made a funny noise that sounded like 'Grumph' but she put food on Oddjobs' plate, and soon we were all eating and too busy to talk, except for things like 'lovely bit of goose,' 'beautiful stuffing,' 'anybody want any more now?' Then the pudding came, smelling rich as the east, and we had oceans of custard poured over it and I found the lucky threepence.

How quickly the day flew by! The grown-ups dozing after dinner round the fire - ladies in the front room, men in the middle room smoking cigars and all sipping at little Miss Williams' Ginger Wine.

Then tea, with Trifle and Christmas Cake and mince pies, then guessing games, and forfeits, and conversation lozenges, and all the time... 'Do you remember when - ' and tales of times of other Christmases went round and round.

Siencyn Oddjobs, good as gold, all 'please and thank you,' and Auntie Bessie passing the peppermints, and Uncle Arthur in the most comfortable arm chair and little Miss Williams very lady-like but getting her share - Oh! How we all enjoyed ourselves.

Then supper, with the goose cold, with pickles and chutney, and a chocolate log, and more cakes and mince pies and gallons of tea, and Billy suddenly remembering he'd brought some Parsnip Wine. "No harm in Parsnip Wine," said Aunty Scissors Ann. "All home made it is." So Mam got out the glasses again.

"What about you?" she asked Siencyn. "Haven't you signed the Pledge?"

"Not yet, Mrs Williams," said Siencyn, taking the fullest glass.

"Parsnip Wine isn't strong drink," said Auntie Bessie, taking some. Then Dadda played the piano, and he and Mam sang duets 'Hywel and Blodwyn,' and 'Trot Here and There,' and little Miss Williams sang that her love was like a red, red rose, and Billy sang 'When Father Painted the Parlour' and Aunty Scissors Ann got out another bottle of Parsnip Wine. I recited a poem called 'Pity the Drunkard's Daughter,' and Auntie Bessie sang 'Red Sails in the Sunset.' Uncle Arthur suddenly burst out laughing and told us a joke he remembered from when he was a boy. This was the first time he'd spoken all day, he forgot the joke half way through and he couldn't remember how it finished, but we laughed all the same.

Then we all sang carols, and hymns and songs, the voices blending and harmonising, sweet sopranos, warm contraltos, Billy's lovely tenor voice, and Dadda and Uncle Arthur's bass. Siencyn Oddjobs had a real good voice and he sang with his eyes shut, lost in his own music. I sat on Auntie Bessie's lap, warm and cwtchy, the few drops of Parsnip Wine I'd had, making me nice and sleepy.

"More wine?" said Billy, bringing out another bottle.

"Bed," said Mam to me. Obediently I stood up. "Goodnight, everybody," I said. Auntie Bessie kissed me good night, I kissed Dadda. "Aren't you going to kiss me?" asked Aunty Scissors Ann. 'There's a change,' I thought, but I kissed her sharp hard cheek and soon I was in bed and my hot brick so nice in the icy cold of my bedroom.

Mam didn't draw the curtains, and I didn't need my candle. Outside, the night was silver, the moon flooding the sky with light and the frost sparkling and twinkling on the roofs of the houses opposite. The sky was crammed with stars, and all was still and silent and Oh! so beautiful. It must have been like this, I thought, when the shepherds left the hills to go down into the valley to find the stable and the little Baby on that first Christmas, all peace and beauty, and love in a poor place.

"There's beautiful!" said Mam as she looked out of the window. "Christmas is magic," I said.

"It must be," said Mam. "For me to have Siencyn Oddjobs under my roof!"

"And for me to kiss Aunty Scissors Ann," I said. "Mam, do you think Siencyn has repented, and will mend his ways?"

"No," said Mam. "He was just lonely, and wanted warmth and company at Christmas, but he'll be back down the Pub tomorrow, and drunk as a lord next Saturday as usual."

From downstairs came the sound of laughter, and then Auntie Bessie could be heard singing 'Champagne Charlie is my Name'. Mam sighed.

"And I'll tell you another thing, I don't hold out much hope of the staying power of the latest recruit to the International League of Total Teetotalers, neither," she said.

CHAPTER 6

NEW YEAR'S DAY

Sometimes, I thought, life is so lovely I feel as if I'm flying. No sooner was Christmas over, and it was New Year.

The first time Mam let me stay up to see the New Year in, I was so excited! We sat round the kitchen fire talking and drinking hot Oxo, and then Mam said it was time, and we all wrapped up warm and went and stood on the front doorstep. There was a bright moon, and stars, and the frost was silver and twinkling and shining on the roofs and the road. Then suddenly we heard it - the Pit Hooter, sounding loud in the clear air, and then the loud bangs from the railway at the top of the street, where the drivers had put detonators on the line, and were driving the engines over them to explode them.

"Happy New Year," we called to all the neighbours who were all standing in groups by their front doors. "Happy New Year," they called to us, and then we went indoors and had a glass of Aunty Scissors Ann's home-made elderberry wine. I was nearly sick with excitement.

The next morning, it was up early to go around the shops for New Year's Gifts. Mam wrapped me up warm, gaiters over my woollen stockings, coat, cap, gloves and a scarf shawl over my shoulders, and crossed in front and safety pinned behind.

"Careful you don't slip on the pavements," said Mam. "And keep your ears warm, and don't drop your basket."

It was still very cold and frosty, and icicles hung from roofs and drainpipes.

I called for Siân, and we started our rounds.

Mrs Wilkins first, we decided. We always spent our pocket money in her sweet shop. The shop bell tinged as we went in. "Happy New Year, Mrs Wilkins. Have you got any New Year's Gifts?"

"No, not this year. Shut the door as you go out." And before we knew it we were back on the pavement again.

"Well," I said. "I'm not going to patronise her shop no more. The money I've spent there, ha'pennies and ha'pennies."

"Me neither," said Siân. "Mean old thing. Now where?"

"Let's try Miss Kinglake," I suggested. Siân looked doubtful, but we thought we could try.

Miss Kinglake was very old and sold Newspapers, and stamps from a tin with Queen Victoria on it, and she wouldn't serve anybody unless they had clean hands, or who forgot to say please and thank you. Her counter was very high, and we were very short. We tried to see over the top.

"Happy New Year, Miss Kinglake!"

"Happy New Year, Children," said Miss Kinglake, "How kind of you to give me the compliments of the season."

There was a long pause. Somehow we just couldn't ask for a New Year's Gift. She peered at us over the top of her steel rimmed spectacles. "Anything else, chidren?"

"No thank you, Miss Kinglake." And we were outside her shop, empty-handed.

We tried Miss Evans, Draper, but her shop was shut. A notice on the door said, 'Opening at 12-15.'

We tried the big grocers, but the manager was standing by the door. "Now then, if it's New Year's Gifts you want - Hop it." We hopped it.

My feet and fingers were freezing, and our breath made white mist in front of us.

Some big boys rushed past, cramming Chelsea Buns into their mouths. "Free buns in Beynon Baker's," they shouted.

As quickly as we could, we slipped and slithered to Beynon the Baker's. As we opened the shop door, there was the smell of warm new bread. Mrs Beynon was putting a large wooden tray behind the counter.

"Happy New Year," we began, but Mrs Beynon interrupted us. "Oh, there's a pity," she said. "All the free buns is gone. Should have been five minutes earlier, you should. Never mind, come back earlier next year."

Once more the shop bell tinged and we were out in the cold, bright open air.

"This is the worse New Year's Day I can remember," grumbled Siân.

"I know," I said. "Let's try Mother Marsh." Mother Marsh kept pigs on her allotment and if you took potato peelings and cabbage stumps to her back door, she'd give you a boiled sweet.

We trailed off to her house. Other children passed us, with apples and oranges and balloons. We couldn't understand why we'd done so badly.

We opened Mother Marsh's back lane gate and called her. After an age of calling and calling, she came to the door, eating bread and dripping. "What do you want?" she asked

Siân nudged me. "Go on, you ask," she said.

"Happy New Year, and have you got any New Year's Gifts?"

"Well I'll be blowed," she said. "Wait there." She was gone so long we thought she'd forgotten us. At last she was back, and gave us each two boiled sweets wrapped in a piece of blue sugar bag. "Don't forget, double peelings next time," she said. "Shut the gate as you go out."

"That's a start anyway," I said. We put the sweets into our baskets, where they looked lost.

"Let's try Shinny Shoes," I suggested. Shinny Shoes was the cobbler, and he mended shoes in a wooden hut stuck on the end of one of the houses. It was shaped like a slice of sponge cake. Over the door was a sign. 'James James: High Class Shoe Repairs'. We opened the door and went in. Shinny Shoes was sitting on a stool, with his last between his knees, putting segs into the soles of working boots. The place smelt of paraffin from his lamp and his primus stove.

Without looking up, he said, "Your shoes will be ready Tuesday."

"We haven't come for shoes," I said. "We've come to say Happy New Year, and have you got any New Year's Gifts?"

He looked up. "Nobody else have been here to wish me the compliments of the season," he said. "I think that deserves something special." From the front pocket of his big apron he brought out a blue cotton bag that made lovely chinking money sounds. "Here you are," he said. "Hold out your hands." Into the middle of each woollen glove he put a new shinning ha'penny - with this new year's date on it!

'Ooh,' I thought. The people in the Mint have been up early this morning to make these in time for to-day!

"Put your money in your glove, now," said Shinny Shoes. We did and the coin felt cold and hard against my hand. "Thank you for the lovely money," I said and Siân said thank you too and then we were off again.

Up the main road again, past Mrs Wilkins' shop. She was standing by her door talking to Mrs Williams Milk. "I'll be glad when it's twelve o'clock. Inundated with them I've been. Happy New Year indeed. Thank goodness only a quarter of an hour to go."

Only a quarter of an hour left and only two boiled sweets and a new ha'penny to show for all our walking about.

"We'd better go home," said Siân.

"Righto," I said.

We walked along, heads down, so as not to fall on a very slippery part, when suddenly we heard someone calling us.

"Come on. Over here. Free New Year's Gifts!" There was a small queue of children and they were standing outside The Club.

The Club was the place that was worse than the Pubs, because it was even open on Sundays. People went there to drink beer, and they could be heard singing on Saturday nights. We had been warned by our mothers not to go near there, and we'd heard in Band of Hope how strong drink was raging there.

"We can't go in there," I said. "We're not members."

"Don't matter," shouted a big boy with a red muffler. "Come in." And we were grabbed and pushed into the middle of the queue. "That all you kids got? Them two sweets," said a girl with pimples and a sniffle. "Let these kids by there, you lot, they haven't had nothing." And we were pushed forward again.

Up the steps we went, our feet hardly touching the ground. This was terrible! If we were found out actually going into the club, we'd be thrown out of the Band of Hope and wouldn't be allowed to go on the outing to Barry Island in the summer. We went along a narrow corridor - I couldn't see where we were going because Siân and I were smaller than the rest of the boys and girls. Suddenly I got frightened. What if they would take me somewhere and force me to drink beer and I would break the Pledge! What if Siân and me were being kidnapped and sent to South America, or South Africa? I went hot and cold all over.

We turned another corner and there in an open doorway sat a fat man with a clothes basket each side of him full of bags of sweets. He pushed a bag into each of my hands.

"Happy New Year. Pass along quickly. Happy New Year. Keep going." We kept going. I put the bags of sweets into my basket. 'Bribery and Corruption,' I thought. We turned another corner. There in another doorway sat a thin man. He had clothes baskets too, one full of apples, and one of oranges. As we passed, he gave us all an apple and an orange. "Come on, come on, Happy New Year." and we walked on.

Now we were going down some steps. My mouth felt dry and I was nearly crying. 'The bowels of the earth,' I thought. This is where something awful is going to happen to me. The children behind me pushed and shoved. I felt trapped. We turned another corner and suddenly we were out into the fresh air! We'd come out at the back of the club! We were safe.

As fast as we could, we got away from there. At the top of our street we looked into the bags of sweets - one was boiled mixture, and one was pear drops. A whole quarter pound in each bag! And the apple - big red and shinning, and the orange a real Jaffa!

"Better not say where we got these," said Siân. I agreed. If Mam knew I'd been in the Club I'd be in real trouble.

"So long," I said, and went home.

Mam was waiting for me. "You're like ice," she said. "Come on, up to the table and get something hot into you. I hope you haven't caught a cold." The broth was lovely and hot, and I got nice and warm.

After dinner, we sat by the fire, Mam and me, sucking the sweets and reading, when Aunty Scissors Ann came in. She plonked herself down on a chair between us and put her feet on the fender.

"Well," she said. "How did you get on?"

"All right, thank you," I said. "Shinny Shoes gave us a New Year's Ha'penny."

"I heard Mrs Wilkins didn't give nothing this year, nor Miss Evans Draper. And fancy, the Club was giving Free Gifts. Shouldn't be allowed. Enticing children to become drunkards, that's what it is."

"Have a pear drop," said Mam. "Megan won't mind sharing." Aunty Scissors Ann took one - a big one. "Lovely," she said. "Where did you get these?" She looked at me, eyes sharp as black needles and mouth like a man trap.

If she guessed where I'd got them - and I knew she'd worm it out of me, I'd be in terrible trouble with Mam. I suddenly had a great idea. "Mam, I've got earache," I whimpered.

That child have always got something," said Aunty Scissors Ann.

"There," said Mam. "I knew I shouldn't ought to have let her go out in that cold weather. Don't cry *cariad*." And in no time, I had a warmed core of boiled onion in my ear and a scarf under my chin and tied in a knot over my head - I looked like one of the Flopsy Bunnies. I was tucked up on the couch with a nice warm shawl over my legs.

"Better let her sleep," said Mam. There'd be no more talk of where I'd got the New Year's Gifts now!

Outside, the weather became even colder, and the gentle darkness fell. Inside it was warm and snug and Mam and Aunty Scissors Ann gossiped and sucked away at the assorted boiled sweets.

As I pretended to sleep, I couldn't help feeling relieved that the two stalwart members of the temperance movement didn't know that the aniseed balls they were enjoying came through the kindness and generosity of the members of that dreadful Drinking Club.

CHAPTER 7

WHERE THERE'S A WILL

The day Ianto Rhys Price Jones was laid to rest, we had terrible weather. Dadda went to the funeral and got soaked to the skin and Mam made him change and put his feet in a bowl of hot water with mustard in it when he came home.

"Why you wanted to go to the funeral of a nasty cantankerous old miser like that, I don't know!" said Mam. "Catching your death for the likes of him."

"Just to show respect, like," said Dadda, as he sat by the fire in warm clothes and ploughed his way through a pound of onions boiled in milk.

"Respect," said Mam. "Respect for that old skinflint!"

"Well Cissie Ann was at the house, helping with the food," said Dadda

"She'd go anywhere for a free meal," said Mam. "I think I'll make up a dose of Life Drops for you when you've finished those onions."

Dadda and I sometimes thought Mam's cures were worse than the illness and I'd rather have a cold any day than a dose of Life Drops. They were so hot they lifted the top of your head off, but before Mam could go to the cupboard for an eggcup to mix them in, the back door opened and in came a gust of wind and rain and Aunty Scissors Ann with a mac over her head.

"Shut the door quick," said Mam. "We'll all catch our deaths."

Aunty Scissors Ann hung the mac up on the hook on the back door. "If I should see the day!" she said. She plonked herself down on the chair opposite Dadda and took her wellingtons off. "I never thought to live to see the day!"

"Come in," said Dadda. "We can all see you've got some news. Let us into it before somebody else beats you to it!"

"Well," said Aunty Scissors Ann. "You know I went to help with the food after the funeral. There was Cadwallader Jones carrying on about the sad loss of a good Uncle and keeping his eye on the ham. Cut so thin it was you could whistle through it. Them two louts of boyos of his were just as bad, but I know they had a crafty fag in the coal cwtch - it don't take ten minutes to fetch a bucket of coal for the front room fire. There's respect, and their poor Maggie Lizzie working in the kitchen till she was nearly dropping - there's a slave for her father and her brothers. Well then, in comes Penry Price to read the will. They had the gall to ask me and Sal Thomas to go in the kitchen, so we couldn't hear!"

"What did you do?" said Dadda. "Creep back and listen at the keyhole?"

"Never you mind what I did," said Aunty Scissors Ann, "But I tell you this, if I hadn't have heard Penry Price, I'd have heard right enough when Cadwallader Jones found out what his Uncle had done with his money!"

"Well, what did he do?" asked Mam. "Old Ianto didn't have no children of his own, and only one nephew. Don't tell me he left it to the chapel - although he went regular he never put more than a ha'penny in the collection. Didn't he leave it to Cadwallader?"

"No!" said Aunty Scissors Ann. "Nor those gallumping boyos of his."

"I give in," said Dadda. "All right, who did he leave his money too?"

"To Maggie Lizzie! Every penny goes to Maggie Lizzie. A proper heiress she is now, and the money invested to bring her two pounds ten shillings a week for life!"

"*Cato'n pawb*," said Dadda. "There's a fortune!"

"That's more than a lot of men earn for a good week's work," said Mam. "And her to do nothing for it! Well if that don't beat all!"

"She'll have all the men in the auction round her like bees round a honeypot after this," chuckled Dadda. "Squint, or no squint."

"Fat lot of chance any man have got to go courting Maggie Lizzie," said Mam. "There's Willie Watkins walking home with her regular every Sunday from Chapel and every Wednesday from Prayer Meeting, and he haven't got further than the front doorstep. Cadwallader Jones don't want to lose a good little housekeeper who don't have no wages. Now she's got all that money he'll make proper sure nobody'll get their hands on her fortune. Poor dab, she's a tidy little worker, although her Teison Lap's like leather!"

Aunty Scissors Ann sniffed. "Willie Watkins is too soft by half. Working for a draper is no life for a man. He ought to stand up to Cadwallader Jones, Insurance Agent or no Insurance Agent.

Well, I can't stay here all night, I promised to call in on Marged Siencyn to keep her company for five minutes. Poor soul, all alone since that Siencyn Oddjobs went to the bad."

She climbed into her wellingtons and put the mac over her head. As she put her hand on the latch of the door, she said to me, "You ought to be in bed hours ago. Your mother spoils you."

And don't forget," she added as she went out into the dark, rainy night, "'Little pigs got long ears'." I didn't like my Aunty Scissors Ann.

By next morning, the news of Maggie Lizzie's fortune was all over the place. We'd never had a real heiress in our valley before, and we expected to see her in new clothes, and going to the pictures and sitting upstairs in the one and threes. The only difference her money made was that Cadwallader Jones and his boys kept Maggie Lizzie in the house all the time, except for shopping and Chapel, and even then she wasn't on her own. Cadwallader Jones and his two boys went to Chapel with her, Cadwallader Jones even went to Prayer Meetings on Wednesdays.

Poor Willie Watkins didn't have a look in.

Then came the day of the International. We were playing Scotland at Murrayfield, and Mam was going to a Sisterhood Rally at Swansea. Dadda was minding me and the house, and had got a new battery for the wireless to listen to the match. We were a bit afraid Mam wasn't going to her outing at the last minute because she said I was looking as if I was going to have a cold, but at last, off she went.

As soon as she'd gone out of the front door, Siencyn Oddjobs came in the back.

"*Swmai*, Mr Williams," he said. "I brung a butty with me to hear the match - you don't mind, do you?"

"No," said Dadda. "Come you in." And in walked Willie Watkins.

"Bit miserable he is," said Siencyn. "Women don't half muck up a man's life!"

"We got plenty of time till the match. Sit you down - Draw up to the fire." Dadda wouldn't have said that if Mam had been there, but it was nice and comfortable with the men smoking and talking, and me playing hospitals under the table.

"What you been learning in school then?" asked Siencyn.

"Not History," I said. Mam had made me promise not to tell Siencyn any more History ever! Is Poetry all right Dadda?" I asked.

47

"No harm in Poetry," said Dadda, so I stood up and started to recite.

"'Lochinvar', by Sir Walter Scott." I knew it all off by heart, all the verses, and I enjoyed reciting it from 'Oh, Young Lochinvar is come out the west, Through all the wide border his steed is the best,' right to the end - 'So daring in love and so dauntless in war, There never was knight like young Lochinvar.'"

"Well," said Siencyn. "Well, well, well. To remember all that! Go far she will. A real head she's got by there on her shoulders."

"Did you understand it?" I asked. "No," said Siencyn. "Not a blessed word, but I did enjoy it."

"It's about this Scotch chap, mun," explained Dadda. "See, he was called Lochinvar, and he ran off with this fair lady. Her father wanted her to marry a dastard, but Lochinvar saved her."

"What's a dastard, Dad?" I asked.

"It's not a nice word," he said.

Willie Watkins said, "Well what did he mean about 'stayed not for brake'?"

"Yes," I said. "And he stopped not for stone, neither. He must have had a stone in his shoe, and he didn't stop to take it out."

"I used to go in a brake when we had outings, when I was a boy," said Oddjobs. "It was like a charabang with horses. This Lochinvar was in such a hurry he didn't stop for the charabang!"

"Recite it again," said Willie Watkins. So I did, but then Dadda said, "Time for the match," and he put the wireless on, and I got on with my game.

It was marvellous to think we could hear the match all the way from Edinburgh. Dadda and Willie and Oddjobs got very excited, they groaned and moaned, then they shouted, "Come on Boys," then they cheered, and then they went quiet, and by half time they were very miserable.

"The Scotch boys have got the edge on us," said Dadda. Then, second half they started getting excited again, and Oddjobs bit his clay pipe so hard it snapped. Then we scored a try. "Convert this," shouted Dadda. "And we win!" Then they all went quiet, and suddenly they were jumping up and down and cheering and laughing.

"What a game!" said Oddjobs. "We beat them, we was the winners."

"A good match," said Dadda. "Our boys deserve to win."

"That does it," said Willie Watkins. "That's made my mind up. We beat the Scotch and what that Scotch boyo Lochinvar can do, this Welshman can do any day."

"What do you mean?" said Dadda.

"I'm not stopping for no charabang either," said Willie Watkins, all excited. "I haven't got a steed, but I got the Great Western Railway. I'm eloping with Maggie Lizzie!"

"Dear Annwyl," whispered Siencyn.

"Go you to Mrs Price's and see if she got a penny for two ha'pennies for the gas," said Dadda, giving me the money. "Hat and coat on, now mind."

I knew they just wanted to get me out of the way - they always made up excuses. Pennies for the gas indeed, when Mam always kept a pile of them in the Coronation mug on the mantelpiece. I went off to Mrs Price next door and she was making bakestone cakes, she gave me one, so I stayed for a bit talking and eating - she'd put too much spice in them, but still, they were nice and hot and had a lot of currants.

When I got back, Willie Watkins and Siencyn were gone, and Dadda was grinning. "No need to tell Mam we had visitors this afternoon," he said.

"All right," I said. I didn't want to hear their old secrets anyway.

Dadda was acting funny for a few days after that. In Chapel on Sunday he just nodded to Willie Watkins as if he didn't know him very well, and he was all over Cadwallader Jones and said a friend of his was thinking about taking out Insurance.

"Send him to me," said Cadwallader Jones. "I'll do him proud. In every night next week I am, except for Prayer Meeting Wednesday!"

Dadda was grinning and chuckling all the way home, and Mam asked him what the joke was, but we could get nothing out of him. He went on like this till Thursday, then after tea, he said he was going out.

"I'm going over the Hall to play billiards," he said. "I'll be back by half past eight."

"Make sure you do," said Mam. "You don't go out usual when you're on nights. It'll be a bit of a rush for you."

Dadda grinned and went out. He didn't often play billiards over the Workmen's Hall, he usually went to the reading room, or played dominoes or just sat around talking, at least that's what he said. Women and little girls never went there, we wasn't wanted.

Mam got Dadda's tommy box ready and put a nice apple in for Warrior. I wish I could have seen Warrior, but he only came up from the pit once a year with the other pit horses for a holiday. Then Mam got the box out with Dadda's pit clothes in, and put it near the fire to warm and get his supper ready. "If he's not back soon," she said, "He'll be late and lose a shift." But punctually at half past eight, Dadda was back, still with that grin on his face, and chuckling to himself.

The next day, the news was all over the place by the time I came home from school at dinner time.

Willie Watkins and Maggie Lizzie had run away together! 'So that's what that funny word meant,' I thought. I pretended not to listen and to eat my dinner while Mam and Aunty Scissors Ann talked all about it, how Cadwallader Jones was hopping mad, and his boys going to thrash Willie Watkins to an inch of his life if they found him. And how Ephraim Evans had seen Maggie Lizzie and Willie getting on the train at half past six - with luggage!

"Good for the pair of them," said Mam. "Teach that old miseryguts a lesson, keeping that poor girl like a skivvy and slavey all those years."

But we didn't hear the truth about it, till Dadda got up tea-time. I was playing hospitals with my dolls. I'd got one ward under the table, and another ward under the dresser and I was the Matron. Mam and Dadda thought I was too busy to listen. They should have remembered what Aunty Scissors Ann had said 'little pigs got long ears'.

"Well," said Mam. "Come on, out with it. You know more about this than you're letting on."

"If I do tell you," said Dadda. "Remember 'Mum's the word'."

"Righto," said Mam. "Though how Willie Watkins ever got near enough to Maggie Lizzie to make any plans to run away, beats me."

"Easy," said Dadda. "Ianto Co-op Bread slipped her a note when he delivered the batch and a Swansea."

"And how did Maggie Lizzie get a note back to Willie Watkins?" asked Mam.

"No need for a note, if she was willing to go off with Willie, she was to hang Cadwallader's blue flannel drawers upside down on the line on Monday," chuckled Dadda.

"*Cato'n pawb,*" said Mam. "You've been seeing too many spy pictures. Hanging the washing out upside down. I never heard such a thing. Well what was the next step in all this excitement?"

"We had to get those two boyos of Cadwallader's out of the way Thursday after tea, so Billy and me asked them to play billiards with us over the Hall - and we'd pay. That did it - mean as muck, and glad to get anything for nothing. We bought a packet of Woodbines, and a bottle of pop each, in Brachi's after the game, so we was sure they wouldn't be home too early!"

"All that money!" said Mam. "There's your pocket money looking small! But what about Cadwallader - he wouldn't leave Maggie Lizzie on her own five minutes. Eyes in the back of his head, he do have. How did you manage him?"

"That was a bit sticky," replied Dadda. "The only way was to get someone to talk to him about Insurance - and if he thinks he can sell anybody a Policy, he'll jaw all night - and he always does his bit of business in the front room. So we sent along somebody who pretended he wanted to buy Insurance!"

Mam was puzzled. "Who'd want to do that, just to help Maggie Lizzie get away from that old devil? I can't think who'd do that."

Dadda chuckled again. "No, you'll never guess in a month of Sundays. Siencyn, it was, Siencyn Oddjobs. Went round there he did at quarter past six, Cadwallader took him into the front room, and Maggie Lizzie went out the back way. She'd hid her case in the coal cwtch, so she just picked it up, went down the back lane, and was on the half past six train with Willie Watkins. Old Siencyn went on about insuring his shack against fire and theft and flood and then wanted a special rate in case snow fell off the top of the quarry on to his roof and brought the lot down. Cadwallader had to look up insurance against avalanches - he don't have much call for that round here - so it was nearly quarter to nine by the time Siencyn went home. He told Cadwallader he'd think about it, and let him know in the morning. He'll be keeping out of his way for a bit!"

"Well," said Mam. "I got to hand it to you, you managed that like in the pictures. I'd rather than a hundred pounds seen old Cadwallader Jones' face when he found Maggie Lizzie was gone. Come on, Bulldog Drummond, you deserve a bit of a treat. I'll open a tin of salmon to celebrate."

Everybody was talking about Maggie Lizzie and Willie Watkins for a bit, then Thomas the Tip ran away with the Rugby outing money and we had something else to talk about. It was some weeks later that Mr Williams the Chemist told Mam the latest news about Maggie Lizzie. There it was in the Western Mail, in black and white and bold as brass - Maggie Lizzie and Willie Watkins married in a Chapel in Swansea!

Cadwallader Jones was so mad, he stopped going to Prayer Meetings and his two boyos gave up Woodbines and billiards for life.

Maggie Lizzie and her money was gone for ever. We heard later Willie Watkins opened his own Drapers shop in Neath, and was doing well. About a year later, Aunty Scissors Ann came in, all of a rush, while we was having breakfast.

"Look at this!" she said. She waved a copy of the Western Mail in front of Mam. "Borrowed this off Mrs Jones Brynheulog, I have. Just you look by here!"

Mam put her glasses on and looked. "Births, Marriages and Deaths," she said. "Who's gone?"

"Nobody's gone," said Aunty Scissors Ann. "But somebody's come! 'To Margaret Elizabeth, wife of William Watkins, a son.'"

"Maggie Lizzie's got a boy! There's lovely," said Mam.

"Yes and look what they're calling him! Lewis Lochinvar Watkins! What sort of a name is Lochinvar? Where did they get a name like that from?"

"Heaven knows!" said Mam.

But me and Dadda did!

CHAPTER 8

ST DAVID'S DAY

"Mam," I called, as I ran into the kitchen after school. "You'll never guess! Our class is going to do the story of Twm Shon Catti for St David's Day Concert and I'm going to be Twm Shon Catti!"

"There's lovely," said Mam, who was busy puttin tea. "What have you got to do then?"

"Well," I said, as I took off my cap and coat and hung them on the hook behind the door, "I've got to be dashing and daring. I've got to rob the rich and give to the poor."

"Like Robin Hood?" asked Mam.

"Yes, that's right," I said. "Robin Hood was the English Twm Shon Catti. I've got to have an adventure, and sing a song, and then we all finish up doing a dance and clapping. I've got a lot to say, and teacher says I've got to laugh debonair."

"What's that mean?" asked Mam, spreading jam thick on my bread and butter, and giving me the strawberry.

"I don't know," I said. "But I've got to practice. And Miss Jones said, I got to wear a Middle Ages outfit, and if she do draw it on paper, can you make it for me?"

"'Course I will, *cariad*," said Mam.

Aunty Scissors Ann sniffed and said, "You spoil that child." But I didn't care. I knew Mam would make my outfit.

We bought the crinkly paper from Mrs Hughes News - she kept the paper shop. My Middle Ages outfit had to be dark green and brown, but Mrs Hughes only had pea-green, and Mam didn't like brown, so she bought a nice pretty pink instead. I had a sort of gymslip thing and a cloak, and a Middle Ages hat, and Mam ran it all up on her machine. I practised my words and tried to laugh debonair, just like Miss Jones had shown me, and at last it was the day before St David's Day.

Mam tried my outfit on me in front of the looking glass in her bedroom. It was lovely, but I was a bit disappointed.

"My hat haven't got no feather!" I said.

"Where am I going to get a feather from?" asked Mam. "I tried to make one out of the crinkly paper but it went all floppy, so you'll have to pretend a feather. Anyway, nobody's going to stop a galloping horse to see if you've got a feather in your cap."

Cousin Billy came for supper. He was having all his food with us because Aunty Scissors Ann had gone to Risca for a bit. Her Bopa Phillips was proper poorly, Aunty Scissors Ann wanted to keep her eye on the sideboard in case someone else got their hands on it.

"Is your Twm Shon Catti outfit all ready for tomorrow?" asked Billy.

"Yes," I said. "It's lovely, only I got no feather for my hat. In the picture teacher gave me, there was a feather in Twm Shon Catti's hat, but Mam haven't got no feathers. It don't look really proper without a feather."

"It'll be all right without a feather," said Billy tucking in to his toasted cheese.

"No it won't," I said.

"There's ungrateful," said Mam. So I didn't say anything else.

As Billy got his coat on to go home, he whispered to me, "Call in at the house on your way to school in the morning and I'll get you a feather. Secret now, mind, not a word to your mother."

He went out, and I felt very excited. It was nice sharing a secret with Billy.

The next morning, Mam put my Twm Shon Catti outfit in a paper frail and pinned my daffodil to my coat. She came with me to the door and waved goodbye. As soon as she'd gone inside, I nipped into cousin Billy's.

"Have you got my feather?" I called as I hurried in.

"Yes, come on," called Billy. I went into the kitchen, and there on the table was a big cardboard box. Cousin Billy opened the box and brought out a lady's hat.

"That's your mother's best hat!" I said.

"I know," Billy said. "But my mother's not here, is she? We'll borrow her feather, and she'll never know."

Aunty Cissie Ann's best hat was like a black straw pudding basin with a thing that looked like the bottom bit of an ice cream cornet, only made of silver, and sticking out of it a black feather. Billy pulled it and the feather came out.

"Here you are," he said. "Look, here's a safety pin. Give me your hat and we'll pin it on proper."

"What if your mother finds out?" I asked. I was beginning to feel a bit worried.

"You look after the feather and bring it back safe, and I'll put it back and she'll never know." He pinned the feather on to my hat and put it back in the paper frail. "Off you go, now, and bring it back now just."

"So long," I said, and went. In the street you could tell it was St David's Day. The other children were wearing leeks or daffodils, and some of the girls wore Welsh costume, or carried frails with dressing up clothes. Some of the boys had wooden swords and cardboard shields, and Johnni Bevan was wearing a crown, with red and green jewels made out of toffee papers.

Billy Phillips called to him from across the road. "What are you wearing on your coat then?"

"It's a leek - what do you think?"

"That's not a leek - it's a gibbon."

"It's not."

"It is."

"Say that again and I'll flip you."

"Come on then, you try it."

But the School Bell rang, and everybody began to hurry. In the playground, everybody was excited and happy. We marched into our classrooms, and after the register, we went into the big hall and sat on the floor in rows, and the concert started.

Our Governess, Miss Wiiliams, had put a big bunch of daffodils in a vase on the table on the platform, and all the teachers were wearing daffodils and nice frocks. We all sang:

The first of March remember,
Is good St David's Day
The patron saint of Cambria
Whose name will live for aye.'

Then Standard I did their turn, and sang a song about the holly tree, and did a dance and verse speaking and then it was our turn.

I had put my Twm Shon Catti outfit on in the classroom, so I was all ready. My feather pulled my cap down over my ear a bit, but that didn't matter. I felt very scared, and my heart was thumping, but I remembered all my words and all my actions and got my laugh right. It was very debonair, I think.

When we had finished, everybody clapped and we went back to our places for Standard III to have their turn. I felt that everybody was looking at me as I went back to sit down, so I hurried, and nearly fell over Jumbo Jones' feet. My cap slipped off my head, Margaret Powell sat on it, and my heart went into my boots.

"Sorry, I couldn't help it," said Margaret, dragging my hat up from underneath her. The hat was ripped right down the middle, but the feather! It was broke in two places. There was no way Aunty Scissors Ann wouldn't notice somebody had been having a go at her feather.

I couldn't see much of the concert, I felt too miserable.

When I got home from school, I called in at cousin Billy's. Lucky it was his day off (he had not long started working at the railway) so I was able to share the disaster with him. When he saw the feather, he groaned.

"Now you've done it," he said. "My mother will skin me alive."

"What can we do?" I asked. "Who do we know might have a feather? What about Siencyn Oddjobs? He do have chickens, and they do have feathers."

"Different sort of feathers." said Billy. "Still, tell you what, after dinner we'll say we're going to take Smot for a walk, and we'll go up to his shack and see if he's got anything. He's a wily old bird, and he might have got a feather. If he can't help, my mother will kill me."

'She will too,' I thought. 'And it's all my fault.'

We always had the afternoon off on St David's day, so after dinner, we put Smot on the lead and went up the mountain. It was sunny, but the wind was sharp, and Mam made me wear my scarf and gloves, as well as my cap that hid my ears - in case of ear-ache - and my coat with the big collar.

Siencyn was smoking by his fire when we got to his shack - the whole place was a fog of smoke - the fire smoked and his pipe smoked and every now and then the wind would blow the smoke back down the chimney as if it wanted to smoke too.

"Watch that dog with my chickens," shouted Siencyn. He grabbed one chicken off the table and another off a chair and shoved them outside.

"Good layers," he told us. "Lay every day they do, I just wish to goodness I knew where they did it. Sit you down now, and have a warm. Spring air is treacherous. Don't catch cold."

"We can't stop long," said Billy. "I got a practice of the *Messiah* tonight, but we was just wondering if you've got a feather like this one you could let us have?" He took his mother's feather out of his pocket and showed it to Siencyn.

"Bit broke, isn't it?" he said. "No, I got no feathers like that. What you want it for, anyway?"

Billy told him, Siencyn spat in the fire.

"Bloody women and their hats and their feathers," he said.

'I'm one of them,' I thought. Then suddenly Siencyn said, "Let me have another look at that feather." He took it in his hand and stared at it for a bit, and then he began to make funny wheezing noises, which was his way of laughing.

"I can get you a feather like this Thursday night," he said. "That do you?"

"Great," said Billy. "My mother's coming home Friday because of the Sisterhood big meeting Saturday, so that'll be fine. You sure you can get the same feather?"

"Certain sure," wheezed Siencyn. "Did your mother buy her hat in the Co-op in Ponty?"

"Yes I think so," said Billy.

Siencyn wheezed again. "I'll get it for you, don't you worry. Fourteen and eleven indeed, there's money! I'll come round to your house about half past seven Thursday night."

"I'll be there," said Billy. "And thanks a lot. Come on Megan. You don't half land me in trouble."

On the way home, I asked Billy what Siencyn meant by '14/11 indeed', but he didn't know, and didn't seem to think it was important.

Thursday night, Mam went to Sisterhood, so Dadda stayed with me, and we played Ludo. About eight o'clock, just when I was getting ready for bed, Billy came in. He winked at me and nodded, so I knew everything was all right. When Dadda went upstairs to get my candlestick from my bed, Billy whispered, "It's great! It's exactly the same feather, and we put it back in that silver thing, and you'd never know the difference!"

I felt so relieved I went to sleep as soon as Dadda cwtched me up in bed.

Aunty Scissors Ann came home Friday - her Bopa Phillips had got better, so she hadn't got her sideboard this time - and on Saturday morning Mam and her went to the Chapel to get the food ready for the Big Tea they were going to have after the big Sisterhood Rally. When Mam came home, we had a quick dinner, then she changed and put on her best clothes, Aunty Scissors Ann came to call for her, and there on her head was her Sunday hat, and the feather was there, straight as an arrow.

"Come on," said Aunty Scissors Ann. "I want a good seat, and the buses will be here soon. Coming from all over, they are," she told Dadda. "And the Chapel will be packed."

"I'm ready," said Mam, and they was gone leaving us in peace and quiet. Time for Dadda to read the paper, and have a little nap, for me to read, and play with my dolls.

It was nearly seven o'clock before Mam came home.

"You look whacked out," said Dadda. "Here, sit you down, and I'll wet the tea."

"I'll just change my best frock first, case I spill something on it," said Mam.

When she came downstairs, she sat down by the fire and put her feet on the fender, and drank her tea.

"That's nice," she said. "I didn't know how tired I was. Been on my feet hours I have. Four hundred teas we did - Oh I forgot - I've got a bit of slab cake in my bag, for Megan."

"Ooh! Thanks," I said. It was my favourite, pink and yellow, with thick jam and pretending cream in the middle, and a real big slice it was too.

"Good Meeting?" asked Dadda, poking the fire.

"Lovely," said Mam. "Very good Preacher, she was, and prayed beautiful. Funny thing happened though."

"Well go on," said Dadda. "Tell us the story."

"It's nothing really, only it's so peculiar," said Mam. "Marged Siencyn Oddjobs was sitting behind us in Chapel, and when we got up in the last hymn to go to the vestry to wet the tea and put the milk in the cups, Marged gave Cissie Ann such a funny look. I couldn't understand it, and then I saw they was wearing the same hats, only Cissie Ann's was black, and Marged's was navy blue and got no feather. Marged was staring like anything at Cissie Ann's hat, then she suddenly said 'Funny you got a black hat and a navy blue feather in it,' and walked off. 'What's wrong with her?' Cissie asked me. 'I've got a black hat and a black feather - always had.' But d'you know, Marged Siencyn was right - Cissie Ann *did* have a navy blue feather in her black hat!"

I nearly choked in my slab cake.

"Perhaps the light was bad," said Dadda.

"No, I had a real good look. It was a navy blue feather. Then I heard Mrs Edwards Mafondy asking Marged if she didn't use to have a feather in her hat, and Marged said, 'Yes she did.' When she put her hat away last time she wore it, it had a feather, but when she opened the box to get it out today, the feather had gone."

I suddenly had a funny pain in my stomach. So that's where Siencyn had got the feather from!

"Mrs Edwards said, 'Perhaps the feather fell down in the wardrobe - the clasp thing could have worked loose. There must be some explanation,' but Marged said, 'Yes, there must be an explanation, and there's those that knows more about it than they let on,' but then people started to come in, and we had to pour the tea, then there was the washing up and clearing away, and I forgot all about it until when we came to get ready to come home and went to put our hats and coats on, Cissie Ann's feather was gone! We all looked for it - Marged Siencyn was ever so kind and looked everywhere - but no go. Where that feather went is a mystery."

"Have to get Sherlock Holmes to find it," said Dadda.

I could hardly finish my slab cake. I wished I'd never wanted a feather for my hat - I wished I'd never been Twm Shon Catti - I wished it had never been St David's Day.

Aunty Scissors Ann didn't go to Chapel on Sunday - had a bad head, she said, and Marged Siencyn didn't go neither.

A whole week went by, and no mention of feathers. Then on the Sunday morning, as we were going into Chapel, here comes Marged Siencyn, in her navy blue hat with the navy blue feather. She nodded to us, and sat in the row in front of us. 'Not feathers again,' I thought.

And then, just before it was time for the service to start, in came Aunty Scissors Ann walking like a queen, in her best black hat with *two* feathers, but not just ordinary ones like before, but two lovely ostrich feathers curled around her hat and moved and gently and softly as she turned her head, a lovely glossy black and a softer white one. You could see people stretching their necks to see, and whispering to their neighbours, and giving each other looks. We were half way into the first hymn before the excitement died down.

After Chapel, we all stood about talking outside, with Aunty Scissors Ann pretending not to notice that everybody was staring at her hat. Pleased as Punch, she was, and enjoying every minute. As Marged Siencyn passed, she called, "Found your feather, I see."

"Yes," said Marged. "It fell down between the bed and the wardrobe. I've put a few stiches in it, so I won't lose it again."

"My feather seems to have gone for good," said Aunty Scissors Ann. "But I've got a good son - he won't see his mother put on - he made me take my hat to Madam Selena Thomas to have it remodelled and the feathers put on, and he footed the bill. I've got the best son in the world."

Madam Selena Thomas! The only real milliner in Ponty where all the *crachach* went to have their hats made special. No doubt about it, that really was a nine days wonder.

As we walked home, I said to cousin Billy, "Did the hat cost a lot of money?"

"Only all my life savings," said Billy miserably. "Saving up to buy a bike I was, but I had to do something or she'd have wormed the whole story out of me, and then the fat would have been in the fire. Twopence, that's all I've got left in the world, a twopence and tonight's collection."

"It's enough for a quarter of coconut mushrooms," I said.

Billy laughed. "All right, after Chapel tonight, coconut mushrooms in Brachi's it is. But next year, on St David's Day, if you as much as hint that you want me to help you with your outfit. I'll wring your neck. Understand!"

"All right," I said, but St David's Day was a year off. Cousin Billy had a short memory, and a heart as big as the sea, and I could twist him round my little finger.

We'll wait and see, I thought.

CHAPTER 9

THE FUNERAL

"Well," said Mam. "That does it. Lizzie May Jenkins' funeral on Saturday and there's no one to leave Megan with."

"Cissie Ann will look after her for us," said Dadda. "Or come to that, I could stop home and mind her."

"I'm not going to Treherbert on my own," said Mam. "And Cissie Ann is going to Risca tomorrow - Bopa Phillips is bad again, and Cissie Ann wants to make sure nobody else don't get the sideboard. Soar Chapel outing on Saturday, and half our Chapel going with them - there's loyalty! And the Church have got sports down in the Vale, so this place will be good as empty. No, there's only one answer: Megan will have to come with us."

"I don't want to go to no funeral," I said, but Mam didn't take no notice.

"We'll catch the nine o'clock bus - that'll get us there in plenty of time. There won't be many at that funeral, I can tell you. Quarrelled with everybody Lizzie May did, but she was good to my mother when I was a little girl and my father hurt bad in the pit, so I'm going out of respect for what she did then. I did hear she hadn't let nobody over her doorstep this year - not even the Minister!"

"Didn't she have a neice that was good to her?" asked Dadda.

"Yes you remember her - Fat Phyllis, good as gold to her she was.

61

Wonder if she'll be there - sure to, never a one to harbour malice she was."

"Tell you who will be going, is Siencyn Oddjobs. He's some sort of relation, a cousin or something."

"Second cousin once removed," said Mam. "He's not coming with us, I can tell you. Shamed before the whole of Treherbert we'd be, with him looking a regular Rodney."

"I'll make sure he comes repectable," said Dadda.

"Make sure you do," said Mam. "Now what can Megan wear?"

I found out it was very important to be dressed proper for a funeral even if nothing fitted.

I had a white blouse with a Peter Pan collar - bit tight, but it was clean and starched and Mam borrowed a Girl Guide skirt and cardigan from little Miss Williams. When I tried it on, it was so big round the waist it slipped to the floor, so Mam took in a couple of lumpy darts each side and kept it up with black garter elastic.

"Is she going to wear black stockings?" asked Dadda

"No indeed," said Mam. "Catch pneumonia she would if she changed back into stockings for one day in the middle of summer. Nice white ankle socks, she'll have and her best shoes is black. Anyway, you won't see much of her legs with her skirt being a bit on the long side."

The cardigan was a bit on the long side too.

"Nothing you could do about that," said Mam, but she took in a tuck at the shoulders and armholes, and turned the sleeves back to make a nice cuff, so it wasn't too bad. I was to wear Mam's black tam on my head - it was a bit on the big side, but Mam put a dart in it, and my best coat, which luckily was navy blue.

The night before the funeral, Siencyn Oddjobs came to borrow the bowler hat, which had used to belong to great Uncle Ben, and had been in a box on top of the wardrobe ever since I could remember. It only came out to be cleaned, once a year.

"Right," said Mam. "Sit down by there, and let me try it on you."

Siencyn sat on the chair by the table and Mam took the bowler out of its box.

"There's a bit of quality," said Siencyn. "I do always think a bowler do add class to a funeral."

Mam placed the hat on his head as if she was the Archbishop of Canterbury and the bowler was the crown of England.

"There!" she said, and stood back to admire it. Siencyn's eyes were almost hidden by the bowler. Dadda began to laugh, but Mam gave him a look.

"Humph, where's the Christian Herald?" she asked. Dadda found the paper under the cushion, and taking out a few pages, she folded them into a long strip and carefully tucked them into the leather hat band inside the hat.

"Try it now," she said.

"It's still a bit loose," said Siencyn, all apologies.

"Your head's on the small side," said Mam crossly. She put some more of the Christian Herald into the hat, and tried it on Siencyn again. This time we could see his eyebrows quite clear.

"Fits lovely," said Mam.

"Bit loose it is still. If I do turn my head, the hat stays where it was, like."

"Then don't turn your head," snapped Mam. "Look, fold down your ears, and they'll stop it slipping anymore."

"Not very comfortable," grumbled Siencyn.

"You don't expect comfort at a funeral," said Mam - really got her moss off by now. I suppose you got a black tie and decent suit ready for tomorrow?"

"I got everything proper," said Siencyn, all dignified he was.

"I hope so," said Mam. "Nine o'clock the bus goes, and if you miss it, you miss the funeral. Off you go now, and remember, tomorrow you *shave*."

Dadda saw Siencyn and the bowler to the front door. I could hear Siencyn whispering something about regular Tartars as they went.

I had to go to bed early, so as not to be tired the next day. Mam made me eat a good breakfast to keep my strength up and we all got dressed in our funeral clothes.

Mam looked lovely, and she had a hat with black shiny beads, and Aunty Scissors Ann's best black coat.

Dadda looked nice too - but I didn't think his collar looked comfortable, although it was white and shining like the Minister's. He had a bowler too - and black gloves. As we walked down the street to the bus we met everybody else going the other way, to Soar Chapel Vestry for the tickets for the outing to Barry Island. They was all dressed in bright clothes, and sun hats, and new daps and had frails of food and buckets and spades.

They all looked respectful at us as we passed, and we looked sorrowful and important. Still I'd have rather be going to Barry Island than a funeral, any day.

Siencyn was waiting for us at the bus stop. I nearly didn't know him! He looked lovely in the bowler, and he had black boots and black trousers and a grey gaberdine mac.

"Well," said Mam. "I've never seen him look so respectable. He can do it if he tries!"

Siencyn grinned and looked awkward, but the bus came soon, and we was all on our way to Treherbert. I sat by the window by Mam, and Siencyn and Dadda sat behind us.

When Dadda showed the tickets, the Conductor said, "Funeral, is it?"

"Yes," said Dadda.

"Near relative?"

"No, old friend."

"Ah," said the conductor. "Sometimes them's the worse."

It was a lovely long ride and I enjoyed it, but at last Mam said it was our stop and we got out.

Lizzie May Jenkins had lived on a side street near the bus stop. So we didn't have far to walk. All the blinds in the street was down, and there was a lot of men in the street in funeral clothes.

"Who's all the men?" I whispered to Dadda.

"Shh!" said Dadda.

Mam knocked at the door quiet like, and it was opened by a fat lady with frizzy hair and a black silk dress.

"Come you in," she whispered, and we crept in.

"This is a sad day," said Mam. "How are you, Phyllis?"

Gosh, I thought, It's Fat Phyllis! Mam was right, she didn't harbour no malice.

"Nice you could come," whispered the lady. "Not many is coming - I'd be glad if Gwyn would go in the front car. No other relatives, see; but the Male Voice Choir have come to show respect."

Siencyn gave a quiet cough. "It can't be - it is! It's Gwylym!"

Who's Gwylym? I wondered, then I saw Siencyn red as a beetroot and looking all embarrassed.

"Swmai'," he whispered, shaking hands with Fat Phyllis.

"There's lovely to see you - you'll go in the first car too. At least we've got a couple of real mourners. I never expected you!"

"Sorry I am I had to bring Megan," whispered Mam. "I had nobody to leave her with."

"That's all right. Stay upstairs, she can, till the funeral's over. Come on *bach*, come upstairs with me, and the rest of you go into the middle room."

Mam and Dadda and Siencyn went silently through the door by the stairs, where I could just see some other people in black, and the lady started to go up - suddenly she stopped.

"You all right, *bach* - do you want to go out the back first?"

"No thanks," I whispered. "I'm all right."

I followed her quietly upstairs. "Here we are," she said. "Stop here in the back bedroom. You don't mind being on your own? Be a good girl, now." And she tiptoed downstairs.

The back bedroom wasn't very interesting - it was mostly bed, with a beige counterpane. Somebody had painted the iron bedstead with silver paint, and it had gone a funny grey colour. There was a chair, and something in the corner covered by a cloth, - I peeped under - only boxes tied with string. I couldn't see out of the window because the curtain was drawn. The room was so quiet! I tiptoed to the bannisters to listen. I heard the front door opening, and the whisper, "It's the Minister," then quiet coughing and whispering, then I could hear the service starting. The Minister went on and on, and people said Amen a lot, then a silence, and peeping over the bannisters, I saw men going into the front room. Another silence, then a whisper, "They can't get the window open! Anybody got a chisel?"

Some whispering, then a thump and a squeak, then, "Mr Edwards have done it. Put his hand under the tap - no it's all right, he have wrapped his hankie round it."

I didn't know what was going on - nobody told me they had to take Lizzie May through the front window because their passage was too narrow. I went quietly back into the bedroom.

Outside in the street the choir had started to sing 'Cwm Rhondda' - oh! there's beautiful they did sing. The top tenors was a treat. They sang the last chorus over again, then I heard the sound of car engines starting and men's boots marching as they led the funeral procession to the Cemetery. I'd like to have seen Dadda sitting in a big car, but I daren't peep through the front bedroom curtain - Mam would have killed me if she'd found out.

At last it was all quiet in the street, and I heard voices - not whispers now.

"I'll put the kettle on."

"Here's a clean cloth."

"Mind the milk."

Then Fat Phyllis called me to come down. "There's a good girl you've been. Come on, we're in the middle kitchen."

What a change! All the men had gone, and five or six women was busy getting the food ready.

"We'll have ours first - the men will take a long time - all the way to Hirwaun they've gone," said Fat Phyllis, and soon we was all sitting round the table, having lovely food. Beautiful ham, and as much pickles as you wanted, and tea by the gallon, and a lovely bit of slab cake.

"I never think a funeral goes well without a bit of seed cake," said Fat Phyllis.

"Lovely spread," said a thin little lady with whiskers.

"Yes," said Fat Phyllis, her mouth full of seed cake. "It's what they calls justifiable funeral expenses."

"Did she have much to leave?" asked a lady with not many front teeth.

"No, I don't think so," said Fat Phyllis, starting on the walnut cake. "House is rented, and the Insurance only covered the funeral. There's only these few bits of furniture, and some of them 'ave got the woodworm."

"Who did she leave everything to?" asked the whiskery lady, blowing on her tea in a saucer. "Quarrelled with you years ago, didn't she? And by all accounts even fell out with the Chapel the last go off."

I like them jugs on the mantelpiece," said Mam. I liked them too, they was like fish with open mouths, and standing on their tails.

"Well," laughed Fat Phyllis. "If she've left them to me, you can have them. Hey, look at the time! We'd better get this lot cleaned up before the men come back."

The women started bustling about, and I felt in the way. I didn't know where to go. So I wandered into the passage and peeped into the front room. It wasn't very bright because the curtains were still drawn, so I took a few steps into the room to see better and I nearly jumped out of my skin. Two big round fierce eyes were staring at me! It was a stuffed owl with a glass bowl thing over it. It had fierce claws and it had caught a poor little mouse that was looking all sad and dead. I quickly went back into the middle kitchen.

There was a little stool behind the big wooden armchair by the fire place, so I sat on it. It was a bit of a squash getting in, because the arm of the horsehair sofa was in the way, but once I got in, it was great. There was more boxes tied with string - she must have been a great one for string, I thought, and an old biscuit tin on the top. The women was too busy to see what I was doing, so slowly I lifted the lid of the tin - and then I gasped! What riches! It must have been Lizzie May's button box, - but what a button box! Not like Mam's, all trouser buttons and shirt buttons and buttons for my liberty bodices, - but red glass buttons like rubies, and green ones, big as shillings, and little silver ones with flowers and coat buttons so big I could hardly hold them in my hand. There was buttons with flowers on them and one lovely button like a pansy with a little sad face.

I scooped them up in my fingers, and the feel of them was lovely. That button box was the most lovely thing I had ever seen.

The men came back from the funeral - not the Male Voice Choir, they was off somewhere, to a Eisteddfod. Mam took their bowler hats into the front room.

"Let me have your overcoat," said Fat Phyllis to Siencyn.

"No thank you, I'll keep it on," he said.

"Don't be daft, you'll miss it when you go out, and it's turning dull outside." Fat Phyllis tried to take his coat off him.

"I don't want it off," said Siencyn, miserably, but Fat Phyllis had arms like hams and Siencyn's coat was off in no time.

"Well," said Mam. "Now I've seen everything. Shame on you Siencyn."

Under the nice grey gaberdine overcoat, Siencyn was wearing his russet red tweed jacket, waistcoat, and trousers. What we thought was nice grey trousers were legs off old trousers, put on over his own, and kept up with safety pins.

"You haven't changed a bit," said Fat Phyllis. "Never mind, you did your best and showed respect. Come and sit by here. Plenty of ham."

Mam looked cross with Siencyn, but nobody else said anything, so the funeral feast went on, and the men ate and talked and the women made tea, and I sat in the corner, finding even more wonderful buttons in the Button Box.

The sound of somebody banging a spoon on the table made me look up. Everyone stopped talking, and a man with a white moustache and bald head coughed a bit, and I heard someone whisper to one of the ladies in the kitchen. "It's Henry Hughes - got the Will!" The lady in the kitchen moved in quickly to stand by the door - everybody could see and hear beautiful.

"Well now," said Mr Henry Hughes - you could tell he was a deacon the way he was important.

"As you know the late Lizzie May Jenkins, whose loss we all mourn –"

"Hear, hear," someone muttered.

"Our departed friend, made several wills during her lifetime, but as she had difference of opinion with everybody in turn, each Will was destroyed and a new one made, with new beneficiaries. The last will she made was witnessed three weeks ago, and destroyed a fortnight later when she had a difference of opinion with the Deacons of the Chapel over the choice of hymns for Big Meetings. As her Executor I was naturally concerned that she might die intestate. However, on going through the papers in the bottom of the wardrobe, I came across an old Will, dated thirty years ago, properly witnessed, and legal - I have taken advice on the matter."

The room was so quiet, you could have heard a pin drop.

"There is one small legacy, and one main beneficiary." Everybody looked puzzled. 'There's long words,' I thought.

Mr Henry Hughes took a spectacle case from his pocket slowly, and pinched them glasses on his nose. He opened a big envelope, and took out a folded paper. Carefully, he opened it, coughed again, and read it to himself. Everybody was leaning forward, hardly breathing. Mr Henry Hughes took his glasses off and put them on top of the paper.

"It is all down in long legal words, which I will read to anyone who is desirous of hearing them. I think, though, it is in order if I tell you what the Will contains in plain words.

"Our departed friend has left a legacy to her second cousin once removed, Gwylym Jenkins, her stuffed owl in a glass case." Siencyn went pink as seaside rock, and so pleased.

"I never thought I'd get the owl," he said. "Always fancied it, I did, till she showed me the door and told me to take my eyes off the bird."

There was a little muttering and moving and Mr Henry Hughes was off again. "The residue of the estate is left to her niece, Miss Phyllis Evans."

This time there was real excitement. Fat Phyllis had got the lot, except the owl! Everybody looked pleased and shook hands with her, and the women went into the back kitchen to wash the dishes. The men went out the back to smoke. Only Mr Henry Hughes and Fat Phyllis were left in the middle kitchen - and me in the corner with the button box.

"Well," said Mr Hughes. "The rent is paid up till next Saturday, but the landlord wants this house for his Aunt, and so you'll have to move this lot by then. No money, I'm afraid, but you might get a bit for some of the furniture. I wouldn't mind buying the sideboard off you, if you don't want it."

'Sideboards again,' I thought. Everybody's after sideboards.

After he'd gone, there was quite a different feel to the place - like being let out of school.

Fat Phyllis shared out the ham and the cake and the neighbours went off to spread the news and put the food in their pantries.

"Well," said Mam. "There's a surprise! Who'd have thought it! What are you doing?" For Fat Phyllis was wrapping the fish vases up in newspaper.

"There," she said. "I promised you should have them if she left them to me - yes, go on, take them."

"Well, I won't say no, if you're sure," said Mam. "Thank you very much. They're lovely."

Siencyn came in carrying his stuffed owl in the glass case. "There's beautiful," he said, "It's a real work of art."

"We'd better get our coats and hats. Time for the bus," said Mam. "Where's our Megan got to? I forgot about her."

"There she is, good as gold, in the corner," said Fat Phyllis. "What you got there, love?"

I showed her the button box. "There's lovely buttons in it," I said.

"Would you like to have it?" asked Fat Phyllis.

"Oooh! yes please," I said, so Fat Phyllis wrapped it up in newspaper, gave it to Dadda to carry.

We was loaded going home. The justifiable funeral expenses was quite a big bag - ham and bread and half a pound of butter, some tea and a big piece of Dundee cake. Dadda carried the fish vases and my button box and Siencyn carried his owl in the glass case, wrapped in an old sheet in case it broke.

He had a job getting it on the bus, the conductor said, "Easy to see you lot been to a funeral!"

Mam gave him such a look!

After tea, it started to rain, and Mam let me play with my button box in the front room. I kept finding new, beautiful buttons I hadn't seen before, and every one was a real treasure.

Just as it was beginning to get dark, the Sunday School Outing people came home. I could see them as they came down the street, their sun hats wet and their daps soaking in the puddles. Mary Williams was crying, and her mother shouting, "I can't help it if you did leave your bucket and spade on the train." And Mam looking through the window said she hoped as how they all wouldn't have pneumonia tomorrow, but she wouldn't be surprised if they did.

All in all, I thought, I was glad I'd gone to a funeral instead of Barry Island, and Mam, fiddling with the fish vases on the mantelpiece, must have thought so too.

CHAPTER 10

TO HAVE MY HEART'S DESIRE

There was a lovely smell in the kitchen as Mam did the ironing. 'Thump' went the iron on the trivet as she folded the pillow cases then a soft swish as she moved the hot iron over the damp starched cotton.

I had the measles and had to stay home from school. As it was so near Easter, the Doctor said I wasn't to go back till after the holidays. My spots had all gone, and I felt all right again, so I enjoyed being home - reading when I wanted to, and playing doll's hospitals, and going out with Mam.

The trouble was, Aunty Scissors Ann seemed to be coming round our house every whip stitch. There's always a fly in every ointment, I thought.

She was sitting by the fire, sucking a Minto and warming her knees by the fire.

"Flowering Sunday, next Sunday," said Mam. "When do you think we should go to the Cemetery?"

"Friday," said Aunty Scissors Ann. "I always goes Fridays. If you go before that, the daffodils are looking pretty poor by Sunday and I wouldn't demean myself to go on Saturday, with last lappers. Friday shows the proper respect, and saves money on the flowers. They shoot up in price Saturday mornings."

"Righto," said Mam. "We'll have to take Megan with us, because Gwyn's working nights and there'll be nobody to mind her."

"What we got to do then?" I asked.

"Scrub the headstone, tidy it all up, and wash the china wreaths," said Mam. "And put flowers as well."

"Why?" I asked, but Mam just said, "Because it's Flowering Sunday," and put the cool iron to warm by the fire, and picked up a hot one.

"Flowering Sunday is another name for Palm Sunday," said Aunty Scissors Ann. "That child do never stop asking questions."

I opened my book and pretended to read. I didn't like my Aunty Scissors Ann.

"Anyway," she said. "I've been thinking about going over to Risca on Saturday. There's something going on there, mark my words. Bopa Phillips don't look too good to me, and I know there's them as wants to get their hands on her sideboard. She promised me that sideboard ever since I can remember; I wouldn't put it past Cousin Gwyneth to put her oar in. Set my heart on that sideboard, I have, all these years. Dream about it sometimes, I do."

I couldn't quite understand how Cousin Gwyneth could put an oar in a sideboard, or why she'd want to do it, but I could understand how Aunty Scissors Ann felt about the sideboard. It was the same way I felt about the big pretend monkey nut with the doll inside it I'd seen in the Penny Bazaar when we went to buy candles. You could buy nearly anything you liked in the Penny Bazaar, glass dishes, cups and saucers, pegs, polish and ZEBO; but one part of the counter had toys on it. It was there I saw the pretend monkey nut - long as Mam's hand it was, and inside was a little doll, with a pillow and a little mattress and a blanket with a blue bow on it. It cost sixpence. Mam said children only had toys at Christmas or Birthdays, but I could save up my pocket money to buy it. At a ha'penny a week, it would be three months before I could buy it. I'd saved up for three weeks. I felt that the doll in the pretend monkey nut was out of my reach for ever.

I asked Mam if I could have it instead of an egg for Easter, but Mam said, "No, you don't have Monkey nuts at Easter, you have eggs and that's final. The idea!"

I felt almost sorry for Aunty Scissors Ann.

On Friday morning, Mam had a bilious attack. There was no way she could go to the Cemetery, Aunty Scissors Ann would have to go on her own, with me to help.

I tried to pretend I had a bilious attack too, but Aunty Scissors Ann just said, "Stop that at once!" so I did.

At ten o'clock, we set off. Aunty Scissors Ann carried the galvanised iron bucket, with the scrubbing brush, bar of yellow soap and two floor cloths. In a cloth bag she carried a pop bottle of cold tea. I carried a fish frail with a bag of Welsh cakes. We were ready for anything - I wore enough

71

wool to have kept a flock of sheep hard at it for a year.

To get to the Cemetry, we had to catch a bus to Ponty and then a trolley bus to Treforest. We clanked down the street, and clanked into the bus and off it again. We clanked to the trolley bus stop only to see the back of it moving off round the corner.

"There," said Aunty Scissors Ann. "We've lost it! If you hadn't dawdled we'd have caught it. Well nothing for it, walk we'll have to."

So we walked, in silence, except for the sound of the scrubbing brush clanging about in the bucket, and the handle of the bucket banging about as if it had a life of its own. At last we reached the flower shop.

"Nearly there now," said Aunty Scissors Ann. We bought a bunch of daffodils, and I carried them.

"There's a price for flowers!" said Aunty Scissors Ann. "Daylight robbery."

There were a lot of other women going the same way as we were, all carrying buckets and fish frails and daffodils. We went into the cemetery and found Dadda's and Uncle Iestyn's Grannie's grave. I stayed there with the cold tea and the fish frail and the flowers, while Aunty Scissors Ann went off with the bucket to fill it with water.

They had black pillars with lions' heads, and if you turned a knob by the lion's ear, water came out of his mouth. It was really lovely, but I never got to have a go. Aunty Scissors Ann said I'd break it.

When she came back, she took her coat off and gave it to me to mind, and put on her pinny, then she lifted up the white china wreaths that looked so beautiful under their glass cases. Three of them, there were. They had little wire mesh frames on them to stop them being smashed. Aunty Scissors Ann wouldn't let me touch them. She washed the glass, then dried it, and it shone beautiful. She had rolled up her sleeves, and got down to scrubbing like a Trojan. I sat on a bench and watched her as she did the headstone and the little low walls. When she finished it all looked a treat.

We put the daffodils in a jam jar by the headstone in case the wind blew them over.

"Now," said Aunty Scissors Ann. "I'll go and throw out the water in this bucket, and we'll have something to eat. You sit by there and behave yourself, and don't start on them Welsh cakes."

The sun was shining, and there were daffodils everywhere. It all looked lovely.

When Aunty Scissors Ann came back, she took off her piny, put her coat back on, tidied her hair, and we sat and drank the cold tea and we enjoyed the food. It was a real treat. When we had finished, we tidied everything up ready to go home, then Aunty Scissors Ann said, "Oh look!

Over there! There's Annie Jones Draper's. Haven't seen her in ages. You sit quiet by there, and I'll just go and say hello to her. Behave yourself now." And she hurried off. I could see her about five rows away talking nineteen to the dozen. I sat on the bench. It was made of iron, and it got a bit uncomfortable.

"What you got there, *cariad*?" I looked up. It was Siencyn Oddjobs, in his grey mac and greasy dai cap. He sat down on the bench by me. "Where's your Mam?" he asked.

"She've got a bilious attack," I said.

"Who's brought you then?" he asked.

"My Aunty Scissors Ann," I said. "She's over there - see?"

"Oh aye, jawing somebody's head off as usual. Want a losin?" he asked. "I've got one by here in my waistcoat pocket somewhere." He fumbled about and gave me a pear drop. It was covered in grey fluff.

"Never mind the fluff," he said. "It'll soon suck off."

"Oh thanks," I said. He was right; the fluff did soon suck off. It was a lovely pear drop.

Siencyn suddenly said, "Hey, half a mo." He took his cap off, and from a paper frail he brought out an old railway guard's cap. He put it on his head, and moved off to where a lady was going to get water from the lion's head. Siencyn took her bucket, and filled it with water and went off with her. I could see the lady give him something out of her purse.

Siencyn came and sat on the seat by me. "Only a penny that time," he said. "Last year I done well, but there don't seem to be so much money about this year. Here, you can have it." He gave me the penny.

"Oh thanks," I said. A whole penny! Now I had tuppence ha'penny towards my doll in the monkey nut.

"It's nice sitting by here, isn't it?" said Siencyn, then, "Watch out, here comes trouble." He quickly put his guard's cap back in the frail and put his dai cap back on. "So long, I'm off." He walked off all nonchalant as Aunty Scissors Ann came back.

"Wasn't that Siencyn Oddjobs?" asked Aunty Scissors Ann.

"Where?" I asked.

"Oh you!" she said. "Head in the clouds as usual. Come on, let's go and get the Trolley bus."

It was nice going on the Trolley bus. You got into it in the middle, not at the back, and we had good seats. We didn't have to wait long for the other bus neither, so we were soon home. I'd got used to the noise of the bucket by now. I supposed you can get used to anything in time.

Mam made lovely hot broth for dinner. Her bilious attack was better, but she just had a drink of slippery elm, in case.

"Meet anyone you know?" she asked Aunty Scissors Ann.

"Saw Annie Jones Draper's," said Aunty Scissors Ann. "Tell you what she said later. Not that it came as a surprise to me, but there, nobody listens to *me*. Oh, and there was Siencyn Oddjobs hanging around there too! That man is fast going to You Knows Where!"

I felt very worried about Siencyn Oddjobs.

The next morning, here comes Aunty Scissors Ann, all excitement, waving a letter, and still wearing her Dinkie curlers.

"Look at this!" she called. "Just look by here! I can't get over it! Just you listen to this letter I've got first post from Cousin Gwyneth in Risca!"

"Sideboards again," muttered Dadda, who was having five minutes before going to bed after the night shift.

Aunty Scissors Ann plonked herself down on the chair by the fire. "Now, let me see - she says she have been poorly with her shoulder again, and Bill - that's her husband - has been bad in bed with a terrible chest, and Cousin Annie's been to Newport to see her mother-in-law - wait a bit - now, here's the bit I want to read to you. She says, 'Bopa Phillips has been poorly all the winter, and has decided to give up the home and go and live six months with me and six months with Emrys and his wife in Aberystwyth. The furniture is to be sold, except for the best bits. Bopa Phillips always said as how you should have the sideboard, so as John James Builder has got to go up the valley to pick up a load of second hand chairs for the Chapel Vestry, he will bring the sideboard and contents to you on Saturday 2 April, and he hopes to be with you about eleven o'clock.' There! What do you think of that! He'll be here today! Cousin Gwyneth was always behind like a cow's tail. Why didn't she let me know sooner? Can you come and help Billy move the furniture round for me, and help John Jones get the sideboard off the lorry. I'm so fussed I don't know where I am!"

"Yes, of course I'll come," said Dadda.

"And contents," said Mam. "The letter said 'and contents', well, what a windfall."

So we all went next door but two to Aunty Scissors Ann's house and made a big space opposite the window. She took the aspidistra and its little table away from the gap in the curtains where it had always been, to stop nosey parkers looking into her front room.

"I'll take this into the middle room," she said. "It'll do better in by there."

"And people can look in easy to see the eighth wonder of the world," said Dadda in a whisper to Mam.

We were ready for John Jones Builder an hour before he was due. Aunty Scissors Ann made a cup in hand, and for once she put enough tea leaves in the pot. We kept going to the front door to see if the lorry was coming, and all the neighbours knew something was up. By the time the lorry turned into our street, all the women were either sweeping their fronts or cleaning their front room windows.

The sideboard was huge! And all covered with sheets. Lucky John James Builder had brought his butty, so the four men got it off the lorry.

Aunty Scissors Ann was in a state! Hopping everywhere she was. You should have seen her face when the men said it was too big to go in through the passage and the front room door.

"Have to take the window out," said John James Builder.

Mam took Aunty Scissors Ann into the back kitchen to keep her out of the way and stop her getting all wound up. We could hear thumps and noises coming from the front room. It took the best part of the morning to get the sideboard in.

It was in two parts, and the top was as big as the bottom. We made tea and sandwiches for the men, then John James Builder and his butty put the window back in, and Dadda and cousin Billy got a lot of boxes and a tea chest from the back of the lorry, and by the time it was all over, John James Builder with ten shillings for doing a real good job on the window, it was two o'clock.

Dadda went off to bed and cousin Billy went to meet his friends in Bracchi's, so me and Mam helped Aunty Scissors Ann polish the sideboard and open the boxes. It was like Christmas Day.

There was a big box on knives and forks. And plates and tureens and lots of little white china pots with coats of arms of different towns on, a tea set with roses, and two big glass candlestick things.

In a separate box were a lot of glass rods with knobs on, and Mam and Aunty Scissors Ann hung them all round the candlestick things and they looked lovely, and when you moved them, they made pretty tinkly noises. Aunty Scissors Ann was so excited, she was nearly crying.

"Bopa Phillips' crystal danglers," she said. "As I live and breathe."

Then tablecloths and things, all starched and clean, and last of all, a box full of red glass horns.

"And the Epergne! I've got the Epergne!" Aunty Scissors Ann undid the newspaper and there was a silver horn thing and it all fitted together. "And not a crack in anything!" said Aunty Scissors Ann.

When we had put everything tidy, the neighbours started to call in on all sorts of excuses: "Tickets for the Drama, and two ha'pennies for a penny for the gas, borrowing half a cup of sugar till tea time." Aunty Scissors Ann welcomed them all, and took them all in to see her sideboard.

They were in awe of such grandeur.

Mrs Jones Number Seven said it reminded her of the Mansion House in Cardiff - she'd been in a Ladies Choir that had sung there once.

Somebody else said it was fit for Buckingham Palace. Everybody was bowled over by the Epergne.

In Chapel the next day, Aunty Scissors Ann sang louder than anybody else, and it was all smiles. After Chapel, when Mrs Williams Mafondy said that Siencyn Oddjobs had been told off yesterday for pretending to be an official in the Cemetery, and for taking money off ladies for carrying buckets of water for them, Aunty Scissors Ann just said, "Well it's just his nature to get into trouble, I suppose," and left it at that.

"Mark my words, he's heading for You Know Where," said Mrs Williams.

I felt very worried about Siencyn.

Then on Wedsnesday a wonderful thing happened. Aunty Scissors Ann came in to see us, all smiles and humming like a foghorn. "Here you are," she said to me. "Present for you." I opened the paper bag, and there it was - my Pretend Monkey Nut with the little doll inside!

"Oh thank you," I said. "Look Mam. Look at my present!"

"I saw you had your eyes on it the last few times we've been in the Penny Bazaar. Don't I get a kiss, then?"

I kissed that bony cheek. "You *are* kind," I said.

"Well you're a good little girl, and I do like to give people presents," she said, and went off singing about getting through this Vale of Tears.

"Give me Brandy for shock," said Dadda. "To think a sideboard could have made such a transformation in a woman!"

"It was the epergne," I said.

"Well," said Dadda, "If I'd known an epergne could do that, I'd have bought her one years ago. Come on, I've got time before I go to work, let's all go to Bracchi's for a glass of pop."

So we did. I felt so happy. Then I remembered my savings. Tuppence ha'penny! A fortune! After we'd had our pop, I went to the counter and spent all my money. Haporth of Mintoes for Dadda, haporth of pear drops for Mam, haporth of liquorice all sorts for Billy, and haporth of strong mints for Siencyn Oddjobs.

The last ha'penny I spent on coconut mushrooms for me. I thought, perhaps, I should have bought something for Aunty Scissors Ann, but there - she'd got her sideboard and her epergne. When you've got your heart's desire, coconut mushrooms don't seem to matter that much, do they?

That afternoon, me and Dadda went up the mountain for a walk.

"Could we go and see Siencyn?" I asked. "I want to ask him something." I had felt very worried about Siencyn since getting ready for Flowering Sunday.

"Why not, *merch i*," said Dadda. So we turned off at the quarry to Siencyn's shack.

He was digging in the earth under his window.

"I'm making a garden by here," he said, when he saw us. "Going to grow rhubarb. Love rhubarb I do, and I'll be able to sell what I don't want for myself."

"You could grow some mint too," said Dadda. "And a few potatoes."

"Rhubarb's enough for now," said Siencyn. "No need to break my back. Come on in and have a spell."

I couldn't wait another minute!

"Mr Siencyn," I said. "I've got to ask you something."

"Anything I can do for you, *cariad*," he said.

"No, it's nothing like that," I said. "I'm worried you're not going to Heaven when you die."

"Who said so?" said Siencyn. "I tell you I am going to Heaven - definite."

"Are you sure?" I asked. I was beginning to feel happier.

"Certain sure," he said. "When I get to the Pearly Gates, I'm going to swing on them. Back and fore I'll go, until at last St Peter will be real fed up. 'Come on you,' he'll shout, 'Stop messing about, Siencyn. Stop swinging on those gates. In or out, make up your mind.' So I'll say, 'All right,' and I'll go in, and he'll shut the gates after me. Don't you worry, I'm going to Heaven all right."

"I'm glad," I said.

My cup was full and running over. Heaven couldn't be Heaven to me, if Siencyn Oddjobs wasn't there.

CHAPTER 11

A LIFE ON THE OCEAN WAVE

I knew something was up when Mam and Dadda stopped talking when I came into the kitchen. Aunty Scissors Ann, sniffed and said, "You spoil that child," and went out of the back door, and then Mam went on with the ironing, as if there was a race on.

"Here's a ha'penny to buy sweets," said Dadda.

A ha'penny on a Wednesday!

Something was up all right. I said, "Thanks, Dadda," and ran out of the room. As soon as the door was shut, I could hear their voices again.

The next day, I knew all about it. When I came home from school, Dadda said, "How would you like to go on a big ship all the way across the Channel?"

"How do you mean?" I asked.

Mam butted in. "Let me tell her."

It appeared that old Grampa Wilkins had a brother living just outside Minehead, and he wanted to see him once again, before he died. Aunty Scissors Ann said that to her certain knowledge he'd been saying goodbye to his brother for the last fifteen years. Mam said that Grampa Wilkins was failing fast, and that this time might definitely be the last; so it had been arranged for Grampa Wilkins' Idwal to take him on Saturday; money saved for the trip and spending money, and all. Now Idwal had gone and broke his leg on the two-to-ten shift. Proper despairing, Grampa Wilkins had been, - but then they'd thought of Dadda, and he said he'd take the old man, and Mrs Wilkins had said she'd pay for me to go as well if I wanted to go.

If I wanted to go! It was the most exciting thing that had ever happened to me in all my life! Dadda brought out the atlas, and showed how we'd go from Cardiff pier, all the way across the Bristol Channel. I felt like Nelson, Drake, and Prince Madoc who'd found America, all rolled into one. I told everybody in School about it on Friday and practised the hornpipe, and was sick after tea, with excitement.

"What am I going to wear to go?" I asked Mam. "You've got to have special clothes to be a sailor."

"I'll see to it," said Mam, and she put my hair in rags, so that I'd have curls and a headache in the morning. I dreamed of wearing bell bottomed trousers, and a sailor's collar, or perhaps knee breeches and a cocked hat, like Nelson.

Saturday morning I was awake early and boiled egg and toast, and then Mam got me ready to go. When she'd finished, I stared at myself in her wardrobe mirror in dismay. Black patent leather ankle strap shoes, best white socks, pink cotton dress with two frills round the hem and puffed sleeves, a fawn cardigan, blue coat, best winter brown velour bonnet, trimmed with orange rosebuds and tied under the chin with a big bow, and a beige scarf shawl round my shoulders, crossed over in front, and the ends pinned together at the back by two safety pins six inches long.

"But I can't wear this!" I nearly cried. "I don't look like a sailor! Nelson didn't wear a brown bonnet at the Battle of Trafalgar!"

"He would have, if Mam had told him," said Dadda.

"Go like that, or not at all," said Mam. "It'll be cold on the sea, and I don't want you catching your death."

"Come on," said Dadda. "Grampa Wilkins will be waiting."

"Have you got everything?" asked Mam, anxiously. She kissed and hugged me, and told Dadda to look after me, and wondered if they were doing the right thing in letting me go.

Dadda said, "Come on, let's go quick or Mam will change her mind!" And we were off down the street. Women sweeping their fronts waved to us, Aunty Scissors Ann poked her nose out of her front door as we passed to remind me to 'Be a good girl now' and then we were at Grampa Wilkins' house. He was wearing his best funeral suit and his bowler hat, and was sitting in the front room waiting for us.

"He's all ready for you," said Gramma Wilkins. She gave him a final brush down with a fierce clothes brush. "God love him," she said. "He've been a good husband to me these fifty-odd years."

We set off down the street, Grampa Wilkins leaning on his stick, Dadda in his best Trilby, and me wrapped in the scarf shawl holding on to Dadda's hand. The last thing Mam had said was 'Don't let go of your father, or you get lost or abducted!' I didn't know what it meant, but I felt there was a lot of perils facing us that summer morning.

We caught the bus to Ponty, and then rose our tickets at the station. I was always afraid of the engine, as the train moved into the station with steam billing out and the noise and the fearful iron wheels.

We got on to the train and had a compartment to ourselves, so I had a corner seat.. Just as the guard was getting ready to wave his green flag, the door opened, and in came a foxy man, in a rust coloured tweed suit and cloth cap.

"*Swmai*, Mr Williams! Hullo, *merch i*."

It was Siencyn Oddjobs. "Siencyn," said Dadda. "What in the name of faith are you doing here?"

"I heard you was going this year with Mr Wilkins - *Swmai*, Mr Wilkins, 'ow be? Well I thought, I haven't been overseas since the Rechabites outing to the Isle of White, so I thought, darro, time I was on a ship again. So I come. Knew you'd be glad of the company like." Lowering his voice he leaned over and whispered to Dadda, "Thought I'd help you with the old gent, like."

"I've got a feeling," said Dadda, "It's going to be a funny day."

Once we were past Taffs Well and sure Mam couldn't see, Dadda helped me out of the scarf shawl and the bonnet and coat and I sat and looked at the fields and the cows until we came to Queen Street Station. Then out of there and a tram to the Pier Head, and the biggest ship in the world, with a funnel and two big Paddle Wheels, and what seemed like thousands of people getting on her.

I held on to Dadda tight and we sat on the deck on slatted seats, and the seagulls flew all about us. The engines started to throb and pulse and the whole ship moved and the waves moved us up and down.

"All right?" asked Dadda.

"It's lovely," I said.

I sat warm between Siencyn and Dadda, between thick tweed and blue serge. Then Siencyn and old Grampa Wilkins went below the deck for a minute, and Dadda and I watched the sea and sky, and saw other ships, and saw the land getting far away. After a bit, I said, "Dadda, I want to go. What can I do?"

"Don't you worry," said Dadda. "Come on, this way." We went down some steps, and there was a lady with a blue overall. Dadda whispered to her.

She smiled and said, "Come with me, love," and Dadda said, "It's all right, you go with the lady." So I did, and got the surprise of my life. They had lavs on the ship! It was very exciting going, and I decided I'd go again on the way back. As me and Dadda went back to our seats, we passed a room where there was a lot of noise, and men laughing and I could see they were drinking out of big glasses.

"Oh look, Dadda," I said. "There's Siencyn and Grampa Wilkins!"

"They're having a cup of tea," said Dadda, hurrying me along, but I knew it wasn't tea - it was beer. 'Fancy strong drink raging in a ship,' I thought.

It was some time before Siencyn and Grampa Wilkins came back to join us on our seats on the deck. Siencyn was grinning, and Grampa Wilkins seemed to have difficulty with his feet.

"Landing any minute now," said a fat man with whiskers, and there it was - *England*!

I was abroad for the first time in my life.

It was very exciting. I felt like a real traveller as we walked down the gangway, and soon we were on a funny little green bus that took us to the village where Grampa Wilkins had lived when he was a boy. It was all very pretty, no pits or coal tips anywhere, but fields with fat red cows in them and hedges full of wild flowers and such pretty cottages, just like on a calendar.

When we got to the village, Grampa Wilkins' brother was waiting for us. He was the spitting image of the old man, best suit, bowler hat and all.

""How bast ye?" he asked. Grampa Wilkins grunted. It seemed that the reunion was all arranged, a quick one in the Nag's Head, then off to visit Cousin George and Cousin William.

We were not expected to share that hospitality and were to meet Gampa Wilkins at the boat after.

"When's the next bus back to Minehead?" asked Dadda. "We'd rather be by the sea, wouldn't we, Megan?"

But it seemed there wasn't a bus till four o'clock.

The two old men disappeared into the open door of the pub, followed by Siencyn Oddjobs at the double.

"See you by the boat," he said, as the swing doors to the Public Bar closed behind him.

We stood in the deserted village street, five hours till the bus, and nothing to see or do.

"I'm hungry," I said.

"Let's go and have a look if there's a cafe around," said Dadda. "We could both do with a bit of dinner."

There was a butcher's and a grocer's and a greengrocer and a saddler and a shop with sweets and papers, but no cafe. We walked on, until we came to a cottage in a garden of lovely flowers. 'Cream Teas,' it said on a board by the gate. We went up the path. By the front door was another notice: 'Way In.' Feeling shy and uncomfortable, we went inside. In the front room were round tables with white cloths on them, and an assortment of chairs. There was a bell on one of the tables, and a notice by it - 'Please Ring.' Dadda rang the bell and a lady came in, in a flower piny.

"How many?" she asked. "Oh, one and a half," and disappeared before we could tell her what we wanted.

"We'd better sit down," said Dadda, and we chose a table in the corner. We felt awkward in somebody else's house - we didn't know her, and there we were, in her best parlour!

She was gone so long that we was wondering if we'd better creep out again, when the lady came back with a big tray. There was a teapot, and cups and saucers, and bread and butter and jam and a dish of cream. She went out quickly and came back with the sugar and milk.

"One and six," she said.

Dadda gave her the money and she was gone again, like a rabbit diving down its hole. There was no sound in the house - I wondered if she was the other side of the door, listening.

"Is this dinner in England?" I asked.

"I think we've come to a place that doesn't do dinners, only teas," Dadda replied. "Come on, eat it all up."

"What's the cream for?" I asked. "There's no tinned fruit."

"I don't know," said Dadda. "I don't know what it's all about, but the tea's nice and hot, and the butter on that bread is half an inch thick and I'm starving."

It was the best bread and butter and jam I ever tasted in all my life, and the bread smelt beautiful, and it was soft with crispy crusts and the jam was full of blackcurrants.

We ate in silence, until the bread and butter plate and the jam dish were empty. The cream still lay untouched on its dish in the middle of the table. No one else came into the room, so when we'd finished, we crept out into the street again, feeling that eyes were watching us, but we couldn't see nobody.

"What do we do now?" I asked.

"We'll buy sweets and a comic, and find somewhere to have a whiff until the bus comes."

So we went into the sweet shop and I had coconut mushrooms and the *Beano*, and Dadda had mint Imperials. We wandered down the narrow road between the neat hedges, until we came to a cornfield. We sat just inside the gate, so as not to spoil the corn. The sun was warm, and there was a soft wind that made the corn go 'Swish, swish'.

"England is very beautiful," I said.

"This part is," said Dadda.

He lay back, with his hands behind his head. It was so peaceful. A bird was singing above our heads - "That's a skylark," he said. "He sings as he flies up to the sky. Lucky dab, always in the fresh air and sunshine. No going down the old pit for him."

"Don't you go down then," I said. I never liked the thought of the darkness underground.

"Got to," he said. "Got to get money for food and clothes and somebody's got to give old Warrior his lump of sugar. You read your comic - I'm going to have a nap."

So all through the sweet afternoon, I read the comic, and ate my sweets, and lay enjoying the feeling of the strangeness and newness of it all.

By and by Dadda woke up, and we went and stood by the bus stop until the little green bus came for us. It was funny not having people about to talk to.

'It's very pretty, but it's awful quiet by here,' I thought.

When we got to Minehead, we bought Mam a jug with 'A present from Minehead.' on it, and some rock, and then had pie and chips in a *real* cafe, and one with other customers and a big shinning urn and waitresses in white aprons. Then we looked at the sea, and Dadda looked at his watch, and the sun went in, and it got cloudy and it got colder.

"I don't like it here no more," I said. "When are we going home?"

"Five minutes," said Dadda. "Look, you can see our boat coming in." By now there were crowds waiting, but no sign of Grampa Wilkins and Siencyn Oddjobs.

"It's like in that song we sing about Excelsior: 'The shades of night are falling fast'.

"That's not the only thing falling fast," said Dadda. "Look at them old flags."

Three men were coming along, two of them leaning heavily on the one in the middle. Siencyn's face was bright red, Grampa Wilkins's was a pale greeny-grey. Their legs seemed to be weak - and their knees kept giving way beneath them and Grampa Wilkins's brother was out of breath and finding it hard to keep them going.

"What in the name of faith's happened?" asked Dadda.

"Scrumpy," said Grampa Wilkins's brother.

He hooked their arms round Dadda's neck and was gone. Siencyn caught hold of a passing lamppost and clung to it. The next minute he was sitting on the floor, his eyes glazed but his lips smiling.

"Look," said Dadda to me. "You take our tickets, and hold them tight in one hand and hold my coat with the other. All right?"

We moved slowly with the crowds pushing to get on the boat, Dadda with his arms round the two unsteady men, each of them clinging to his neck and me walking behind and hanging on to his coat tails and the tickets for dear life.

When we got on board, they slumped onto the seats, propping each other up. Dadda wiped his forehead with his hankie. I sat between Dadda and a lady in a red floppy sun hat.

"They've had a skinful," she said cheerfully.

The boat was crowded, and soon the big paddles started going and the throbbing and the noise was loud and we were off. It was much colder by this time, and Dadda tied me back up in the scarf shawl, and put my bonnet back on. It was squashed where Siencyn had sat on it - Mam would have something to say about that!

As soon as we left the shore the lady started to rummage in the two fish frails she had.

"Sea air do always give me an appetite," she said. "I've still got a lot of sandwiches left." Grampa Wilkins made a funny noise - Dadda jumped up, grabbed him and ran with him to the side of the ship.

"Not that side," shouted a man in a peaked cap. Dadda stopped, turned, pulled Grampa Wilkins into a sideways gallop and propped him over the rail.

"He's going to drown Grampa Wilkins," I cried. "Don't drown him Dadda."

"'S all right," said the lady. "Only enjoying the view, he is."

In a couple of minutes, Dadda brought him back to his seat, mopping him up with his hankie.

Grampa Wilkins looked very pale, and he shut his eyes, and held on to his walking stick with both hands.

"Want a sandwich?" said the lady to me. "I got lots here. Salmon and ham, what do you rather?"

There was that funny noise again, only this time from Siencyn.

"*Cato'n Pawb*," said Dadda jumping up. He rushed Siencyn to the rail.

I watched while the lady undid the greaseproof paper round the sandwiches. "Help yourself," she said, so I did.

I was nice and warm, cwtched up to the lady's woolly cardigan, while we ate our way back to Cardiff. After the sandwiches we had welsh cakes, and slab cake and fruit cake, and then a bar of chocolate and a bag of pear drops.

Grampa Wilkins and Siencyn went a few more times to admire the view, and I went with the lady down the steps to the boat's lavies I couldn't miss a treat like that.

Dadda was looking very worried. He was talking to the man in the cap and muffler next to him.

"Them old flags have been at the scrumpy that this cousin George made on his farm - and that on top of a couple of pints of Brains Dark and goodness knows what they had at the *Nags Head*."

"How far are you going with them?" asked the man. "I'm going to Porth myself, any use to you, butty?"

"We're going to Ponty. I'd be glad of a hand with them," said Dadda.

It was easier getting off the boat, because the man in the muffler looked after Siencyn, and the lady looked after me, and so Dadda only had to look after Grampa Wilkins.

We got on the tram at the Pier Head and rattled along to Queen Street Station. The tram swayed about a bit at one point, and Grampa Wilkins made the funny noise, but it was all right.

The steps up to the platform were a bit tricky. Grampa Wilkins seemed to have three legs, and he got his stick caught between Dadda's feet and they nearly fell, and Siencyn wanted to sit down and close his eyes and sing 'Calon Lan', but we got them on the train all right. Grampa Wilkins went to sleep in the corner, but Siencyn got a bit noisy.

"I'll fight anybody in this train," he said. "I'll go six rounds."

He stood up and squared his fists and fell over and woke Grampa Wilkins. The lady began to rummage in her fish frails again, rustling greaseproof paper.

"I wouldn't, if I was you," said Dadda.

"P'raps not," laughed the lady.

"Tell you what," said the man in the muffler. "I'll get off the train at Ponty, and come on the Porth bus with you. I can give you a hand with one of them, and you won't have far to walk on your own with them, will you, while I stay on the bus and get off at Porth Square."

"Thanks, butty," said Dadda. "You're a real Samaritan."

He doesn't look like the picture in the Bible, I thought, either he ought to be wearing a headdress thing and long frock, or the man in the Bible picture ought to be wearing a muffler and a Dai cap.

By the time we got on the bus, Grampa Wilkins and Siencyn had gone quiet, they leaned their heads against the windows, and stared with eyes like dead herrings straight in front of them.

At our bus stop the Samaritan and the conductor helped us off. Dadda grasping the two Zombies, with me still holding on to his coat tails for fear I'd get lost or abducted or both, walking behind.

It was not easy. Grampa Wilkins walked like a jerky toy soldier, and Siencyn kept wanting to lie down on the pavement. At last Dadda had had enough.

"Look," he said to me. "We'll go up our back lane, and put Siencyn in our coal cwtch while we take Grampa Wilkins home. Lucky we haven't met anybody so far, but if Mam or Gramma Wilkins sees Siencyn in this state, the fat will be in the fire." We walked up the lane.

"Thank goodness, Mam haven't bolted the back lane gate," he said. We propped Grampa Wilkins up against the wall, while we got Siencyn into the coal cwtch. He flopped on to the small coal and was sleeping in no time.

"He'll have to stay there all night, unless I can get our Billy to take him home," said Dadda.

"He'll catch his death," I said.

"Not with all that Harris Tweed on, and he's put his best wool vest and long pants on to go on the outing in case he was run over. Eskimos don't wear more than he's got on," replied Dadda.

We left him there, and quietly closed the coal cwtch door and the back gate and walked back down the lane, turned the corner into our street and ran into the reception committee. Gramma Wilkins was standing on her front door step, with Mam and Aunty Scissors Ann.

"God love him, there he is," said Gramma Wilkins. "Gwyneth, here's Dad home." And he was bundled inside with a lot of: "There's lovely he's back." "Tired he do look." "Bed's the best place."

"Come you all in," said Gramma Wilkins. "Have a cup in hand, and I can thank you proper for taking him to see his poor brother for the last time."

So we all went inside and had tea and sandwiches, while Grampa Wilkins was bustled upstairs and washed and undressed and rolled into bed.

"'ave he been bad on the ship?" asked Gramma Wilkins.

"Bit sea sick. Rough crossing," said Dadda, staring hard at me, and filling my mouth with cake.

"Bless the dear soul, he do always have to stay in bed the day after he been to Minehead. He do take the parting awful bad."

Grampa Wilkins' Idwal was lying on the couch with his leg in plaster. "Sad I was I couldn't go," he said.

Mam and Aunty Scissors Ann went into the back kitchen to help Gwyneth wash up, while Gramma Wilkins saw to her husband. Dadda didn't notice me quiet in the corner. "Sad you were, my foot," said Dadda. "Knowing what I do know, it wouldn't surprise me you didn't break your leg on purpose not to take him. You knew what you was letting me in for."

Idwal chuckled. "Every year it's the same. Cousin George's scrumpy, on top of beer on the boat and ale in the *Nags Head*. Paralytic he is by the time I do get him home. Poor old dab, just once a year on a spree away from Mam and Auntie Gwyneth - can't blame him, can you?"

"And does Siencyn Oddjobs always come too," asked Dadda.

"*Darro*, *he* didn't go with you, did he? *Jawch*, you've had it worse than ever I had it. He never came with me before. You deserve a medal."

"Thank *you*," said Dadda. "You could have warned me, anyway, not letting me go and have the trouble I did."

"Well, you'll know better next time - know what to expect, like. My leg will be weak for years yet, and the old man really likes you. How's about doing me a real favour. How's about taking him to say goodbye for ever, again next year?"

Dadda *looked* that's all he said, but next year, when Grampa Wilkins went to say goodbye to his brother, Dadda had lumbago awful bad. We stood on the door and watched Idwal and his father setting off for foreign ports, Dadda moaning and groaning from the pain. But a funny thing, as soon as they was out of sight round the corner, Dadda's back suddenly got better.

"I'm off up the allotment," he told Mam, and went off whistling 'A life on the Ocean's wave', as chirpy as you like.

"Pity his back didn't get better sooner, he could have gone to Minehead," I said, but Mam just laughed.

CHAPTER 12

THE SUNDAY SCHOOL OUTING

We were playing in Nanci Powell's chicken's cwtch - the chickens had gone a long time ago, and green leaves with pretty white flowers grew all over the wire netting. It made a lovely house, and we were having a good game, Nanci, Gwyneth, Siân and me, when Mrs Powell called us into the kitchen.

"Come and see what I just bought," she said. On the table was a brown paper parcel - she untied the string, and let Nanci open it.

"Oooh! There's lovely." Four pairs of eyes stared at the bright yellow frilled net - yards and yards of it.

"It's for Nanci's dress for the Anniversary," Mrs Powell told us. "See there's these frills, they do make the skirt of the frock, and this plain net bit by here, that do be making the bodice and puff sleeves. This yellow crepe de sheen is for the underneath. And look at this lovely trimming all along the frills - little yellow rosebuds. What do you think of that then?"

We all felt sick with envy. The thought that Nanci would be clothed in splendour, while she said her recitation in the Chapel, was like wormwood and gall to us.

"They got it in pink and blue as well - in the *Co-op* in Market Square. Off you all go home now - we're going to have our tea." And Mrs Price wrapped the material up again and put it on top of her sewing machine.

We didn't talk to each other going home. The yellow net with frills floored us completely.

As soon as I got home, I told Mam about it. "Nanci Powell's going to wear yellow net with frills for the Anniversary and it's got rosebuds and puff sleeves, and they've got it in pink and blue as well, in the *Co-op* and can I have the pink net, with rosebuds and frills?"

"Rosebuds and frills indeed!" said Mam as she cut bread and butter for tea. "It's a Sunday School Anniversary, not an Operetta. No, I've seen some nice plain pink crepe de sheen in the Co-op, and Mrs Williams Top House, lent me a pattern. We'll go and get the material Friday after you come home from School."

"Oh, but Mam," I began.

"No argument," said Mam. "Wash your hands and come up to the table. You ought to be grateful to have a nice new frock. Yellow net - out of place in a Chapel, that's what I say."

Thus it was that on the Sunday morning of the Anniversary I put on my nice plain pink dress, and my white socks and ankle strap shoes - and felt miserable.

Gwyneth in blue with a white collar, and Siân in green with two frills round the bottom of her frock, came to call for me, and the three of us went to call on Nanci. We tried to cheer each other up.

"There's a pretty colour your frock is." "There's nice your frills do look." "Crepe de sheen is lovely material."

It was no use, of course. Nanci was arrayed like Solomon in all his glory. Not only did the skirt of yellow net consist entirely of rosebuded frills, but there were frills round her neck, and on her puff sleeves. She was wearing yellow socks and silver dance shoes, and had a yellow ribbon in her hair. Mrs Powell was just putting down the curling tongs when we arrived, and the smell of singed hair was strong.

"What do you think of Nanci's dress then?" asked her mother.

"It's lovely," we said. We hated her - we thought she looked so marvellous.

"Just a finishing touch, like," said Mrs Powell, and she patted Nanci's face with her powder puff.

We were aghast. How much more perfect could this outfit be?

"Here's your collection," she added, and tying a ha'penny in a knot in the corner of her hankie, sprayed it and Nanci with Devon Violets scent! It was the last straw.

We followed Nanci out the house and along the road to Chapel.

Other girls in groups chatted happily and showed off their new frocks -

but when they saw Nanci, they were stunned into silence.

It was frightening sitting on the platform, looking at a sea of parents and Chapel goers. Mam and Dadda and Aunty Scissors Ann were in the third row - cousin Billy was up in the gallery with his friends. They nodded and smiled at me - I was too rigid with fear to acknowledge them.

We sang our songs, and said our recitations - I sang a song about being a sunbeam. I'd have been a better sunbeam in yellow net, I thought. And I recited some verses and then the Sunday School Superintendent announced the Sunday School Outing next Saturday, 'God willing.'

My heart jumped - to see the sea - the once a year glimpse of the sea and the sand and the rocks and the fair - and then it plummeted down. I knew as sure as Fate that one year I would get lost on the Sunday School Outing. I just knew it! The crowds of children and parents and the fierce train, and all the other Sunday Schools on the huge beach at Barry Island - all this filled me with a mixture of terror and joy.

Six days to go, I thought, and then I'd see the sea.

After tea, on the Thursday before the Outing the Mothers and Fathers had to go to the Chapel Vestry to buy their tickets. Mam and Aunty Scissors Ann went to get theirs and Dadda's and Billy's. When they came back, I could see they were a bit upset.

"Who'd you think was there buying a ticket, bold as you like and shameless?" Mam asked Dadda.

"I dunnow," said Dadda. "Go on, surprise me."

"Siencyn Oddjobs! Siencyn Oddjobs never puts his foot inside a Chapel from one year's end to another, and buying a ticket for the Sunday School Outing!"

"Shouldn't have been allowed," snapped Aunty Scissors Ann. "The Deacons did ought to have stopped him. There's cheek he do have - cheek of the Devil."

"No harm in old Siencyn," said Dadda. "Lonely he do get - no chance any other way for company or an Outing to Barry Island!"

"Tut, tut, tut!" said Aunty Scissors Ann. "Company enough he'd get if he went back to live with his wife - a tidier little woman never breathed - and there he is, up in that shack on the mountain, up to no good all the time. Don't talk to me about Siencyn Oddjobs."

The next day, all the Sunday School Scholars went to the Chapel Vestry to get their tickets - our names were crossed off a big list as we were given pieces of cardboard with the Chapel Stamp on them. We carried them home carefully - what if we lost them and couldn't go on the Outing?

At home, Mam was getting the food ready to go. The Welsh cakes were cooling on the kitchen table, and Mam was just taking the Teisen Lap out of the oven. Slices of cooked ham and tomatoes were keeping fresh on the stone slab in the pantry. There was a big bottle of Corona pop, and the Thermos flask, the tin for the sugar and three odd cups were put out for the morning ready. We took enough food with us to last for the outing, and a bit more in case.

I never knew what the 'In case' meant, but it was comforting to know we couldn't starve if the train didn't come to fetch us home at the end of the treat.

The next morning we were all up early. Mam made the sandwiches and Dadda packed the food in a basket and a frail with 'Jones's Fish' on the sides. I had my bathers wrapped in my towel, and my bucket and spade, and I had a new pair of daps to go. I was so excited I was nearly sick.

We had to be at the Chapel at half past nine, so we left home to walk the two hundred yards at nine o'clock.

We children sat in the Vestry with our teachers, all laughing and talking and joking - all except me. I knew I was going to get lost. I'd never see my mother and father again - I'd end up living in the Lost Children's Pound behind wire netting, until I became old and died - I clutched my bucket and spade for comfort.

At last we were ready to go. In twos, we climbed up the steps to the street, and started walking to the station. People came out to see us, and waved to us. Mam and Dad walked on the opposite pavement waving and calling to me. We marched through the booking hall and up the steps to the platform. As we went through the barrier, the ticket collector and the Sunday School Superintendent counted us.

Inside the barrier, Mam and Dad were anxiously watching for me - at last, we were free to find our parents. I felt like the people who had been at the Relief of Mafeking must have felt.

The next fear I had to overcome was the arrival of the train. The engine with its smoke and steam and noise was an object of terror mixed with fascination.

I hid behind my father, while the monster rushed into the station. What if it jumped off the rails onto the platform and landed on all of us? A sigh of relief - it was all right - the train had stopped, and we all rushed to get on. Billy first, then Mam holding my hand and the bag with the bathers, then Aunty Scissors Ann and the basket and an umbrella, then Dadda with the fish frails and a bag of bananas. We had an empty compartment all to ourselves, and I had a seat by the window. One of Billy's friends got on, then suddenly, there was Siencyn Oddjobs, grinning like a fox in his best

Harris Tweed suit and cap.

He sat next to Dadda. *"Swmai?"* he said. "Lovely day for the treat." He carried a leatherette bag, with a pop bottle of cold tea sticking out at the top.

Aunty Scissors Ann looked daggers, but the guard was slamming the train doors, and blowing his whistle and waving his green flag and we were moving - we were off! Off to Barry Island!

All along the train we could here children cheering and shouting.

I hadn't got lost, and I had a seat by the window and the sun was shining and my new daps looked lovely and I was happy as the Queen of Sheba. (Nanci Powell hadn't got new daps, and that nearly made up for the yellow net and frills.)

It was lovely looking out of the window. I loved seeing the cows and horses in the fields and little copses of trees, and once a man on a bicycle waved at me, but best of all I loved it when we chuffed past people's back gardens, and we could look at women hanging out their clothes, or children playing in the grass. These houses were ever so posh, and we were able to have quick looks into their windows as we passed.

Mam let me have more dolly mixtures too - it was a wonderful treat altogether.

At last we heard a burst of cheering from other compartments cries of, "The Sea. There's the sea!"

"Where is it?" I asked. Dadda let me lean out of the window to look at the ribbon of silver ahead, that was the sea, then Mam made me sit down again in case I had a cinder from the engine in my eye.

In no time at all, we were at Barry Island. The train stopped, and shouting and talking and laughing and pushing we got off the train. I held tight to Dadda and my bucket and spade, and we got off the platform and walked to the beach.

The air smelled different, cool and clean and salty. Aunty Scissors Ann was giving Siencyn Oddjobs very funny looks, but he still didn't seem to notice and came with us.

As soon as we'd walked down the slope to the beach Mam let me take my daps and socks off, and the sand was warm and dry between my toes.

We had a job to find somewhere to settle, on that beach it was so crowded, but at last we found a nice space. Dadda and Billy went off to get the deckchairs, and Mam let me put my bathers on.

The sun was warm and there was only a little breeze. Mam and Aunty Scissors Ann sat in deckchairs and Dadda and Billy helped me make a sand castle and dumplings. Siencyn sat on the sand by us and drank from his bottle of cold tea.

"Can I go swimming?" I asked, and Dadda said we'd better go now before we had our sandwiches, so he rolled up the legs of his trousers over his knees, and Billy changed into his bathers. They were very smart ones, with black on the bottom and red and white stripes on the top and a big ring cut out each side.

"Hold Dadda's hand now," said Mam, so I did and we went down to the sea. Oh! the water was cold! At first I let the sea run over my feet, then I went in up to my knees. Billy was swimming and showing off, and then he came and held my hand and we walked out deeper.

"I'll show you how to swim," he said and he put his hand under my chin, and I splashed my legs and felt very proud of myself. Then Dadda said I'd been in long enough and we ran back to Mam, and she wrapped me in the towel and dried me and I shivered and was glad to get my clothes on.

"Now," said Aunty Scissors Ann. "Eat up everybody." And we ate the sandwiches and cake and Dadda sent to the place where it said, 'Trays for the beach,' and brought a pot of tea and cups and saucers and everything.

"This is the life," said Mam. Siencyn didn't say anything - he was lying with his hands behind his head, and his cap over his face.

A man came along the sand selling comics, and Mam bought one for me - it had a free gift with it, an aeroplane you could make yourself.

"Let's make a moat for the castle," said Dad. So we did, then we went down to the sea with my bucket to get water. Mam made me tuck my clothes in my knickers to keep my frock dry in case the waves splashed me. We brought pebbles back too, for my castle, and then Billy took me down to get another bucket of water, to make the moat deeper - the first lot of water had just disappeared into the sand.

"Oh look!" I said. "Seaweed!" A long strand was floating on top of the waves. I stretched to reach it and slipped into the water. I was soaking!

"You'll cop it," said Billy. "Your Mam's going to get her moss off when she sees you."

We hurried back up the beach. "Mam," I wailed. "I fell in."

"You naughty girl," said Mam. "And us with nothing to change you into. Your bathers is soaking wet. Still, come on, out of those wet clothes. We'll have to wrap you up until your clothes get dry."

Aunty Scissors Ann spread my clothes out on a deck chair, and Mam put me in the long tube of towelling with a string round the neck that we changed under.

"I can't play like this," I said. My arms were inside, and my feet hidden by another yard of towelling that flopped on the sand.

"It's your own fault," said Mam. "You could have got drowned."

I sat miserably on a deck chair while Dadda and Billy played cricket with some people from another Chapel who were next to us.

"It's not fair!" I said. "I want to make dumplings. I could only play with my bucket and spade once a year, and here I was, like a captive cocoon watching everybody else enjoying themselves.

"Tell you what," said Aunty Scissors Ann. "I don't feel like going into the sea after all - a little paddle is all I want, so Megan, you can wear my bathers."

"She'll be lost in them," said Mam. I wasn't very keen on the idea either, but it was either stay where I was till all my clothes were dry or try the bathers.

Aunty Scissors Ann's cotton bathers were dull blue on top and grey black on the bottom, and had stretched into a very funny shape. The legs came down to my ankles and the neck line was round my waist.

"She do look indecent." said Mam, but Aunty Scissors Ann took some safety pins from her handbag and lifted the neck line up a foot or so and pinned the shoulders, so that I had long floppy bits hanging down behind.

"There, that'll do," she said.

"It don't look right," said Mam. "But I suppose it'll do till her things dry."

I felt very uncomfortable and knew what I must look like (good job Nanci Powell couldn't see me now, I thought), but at least I could play, and dig in the sand.

The afternoon wore on, Mam and Aunty Scissors Ann were dozing in the deckchairs, Dadda and Billy were still busy with the cricket and Siencyn Oddjobs woke up.

"There's a lovely castle you got there," he said. "And a moat and all. No water in it, though, is it?"

"It went down the sand," I said. "I ought to get more, but everybody's busy, and I mustn't go to the sea by myself."

"I'll come with you," he said. "Enjoy a bit of a paddle, I do."

He rolled up his trouser legs and his woollen pants to his nobly knees, and took off his shoes and stockings.

"Come on, I'll look after you."

I was a bit doubtful, but it wouldn't do any harm - I'd be with a grown-up, and I didn't want to wake Mam or my Aunty. "All right then," I said, and we picked our way to the edge of the sea, between people and sand castles and sunbathers. We seemed to have much further to go than before - "Tide's out," said Siencyn. We filled the bucket with water and pebbles and pretty shells and had a paddle. "It do do the rheumatics good, do salt water," Siencyn told me. "We'd better be getting back."

I turned away from the waves, and looked at the beach. My stomach had a sharp pain and my heart dropped.

There were millions of people on the beach - millions and millions of little coloured dots, and each one was somebody's family - but where, oh where was Mam!

"Which way do we go?" I asked Siencyn.

He scratched his head, and looked around, "I dunno," he said. "This way, I think."

We set off - I didn't want any water in my bucket for the moat, nor pebbles nor sand. I wanted my mother. We blundered around the beach for what seemed like hours. We were lost; I knew we were lost!

"Where do we go now?" I cried. "I want my mother."

"Don't cry, for pity's sake," said Siencyn. "Look here, I tell you what, we'll go to the shelter and then we'll be able to see better. Soon find them, we will."

Slipping and sliding in the hot dry sand, I followed Siencyn to the big shelter on the Promenade. There were a lot of people there, some on deck chairs, some fetching tea, or buying chips, or crisps and rock.

"Now," he said. "We'll stand by here and look down the beach, and we'll see them, don't you worry."

We looked. We looked up the beach and down the beach and from side to side. How in all those crowds of people, could we find Mam and Dad. I gave up all hope, burst into noisy tears and yelled, "I want my mother."

A woman with sticks of rock in her hand stopped and said, "What's the matter *fach*?"

"She've got lost," said Siencyn.

"Oh, God love her," said the woman. "Take her to the lost children's pound - they'll look after her."

"Not the pound," I cried, and bawled louder. A crowd gathered round us. I could hear them say, "What's wrong?"

"Little girl lost."

"Poor little mite."

"Fetch the St John's."

"Tell the Police."

I didn't want the St John's or the Police. I wanted Mam.

Suddenly, Siencyn said, "Don't cry *merch i*. Look, here's a ha'penny."

He pushed a ha'penny into my hand. I was so surprised I stopped crying.

95

"Here you are love," said another man and gave me a penny. Quick as a fox, Siencyn had his cap off and was taking up a collection.

"What's it for?"

"Little girl lost."

"Oh, love her, here's a penny - got any change, Ianto?"

Tear-stained and frightened, I stood a pathetic sight in my strange garment and sand covered feet, while people put money clinking into Siencyn's cap.

Suddenly I heard a voice. "There she is." I looked up - there was Aunty Scissors Ann - My Lovely Aunty Scissors Ann - She caught hold of me and kissed me, then smacked my bottom and said, "You naughty girl. Where have you been? We've been worried to death!"

Relief flooded over me, and I burst into tears again.

"Poor little mite," I heard someone say. "You think they'd have give her better bathers than that!" Aunty Scissors Ann glared at them, grabbing me and my bucket with an iron hand, lead me weeping and wailing back to the beach.

Siencyn had disappeared the moment Aunty Scissors Ann arrived - and so had the money in my hand, but I didn't care. Soon Mam was kissing and hugging me, and I was dressed in my own clothes again and fed and fussed over. Billy and Dadda, who had gone to look for me, came back, and had to be told that Aunty Scissors Ann had found me, in the shelter, and what the woman had said about my bathers, and what Aunty Scissors Ann nearly said back to her.

By now, the sun was getting low in the sky, and people were leaving the beach and going to the fair. We packed up our baskets and fish frails and bathers and Billy and Dadda took the deck chairs back.

"What about Siencyn's boots and stockings?" I asked. They were where he'd left them, when we went to the sea.

"I'll see to them, don't you worry," said Billy. "You go on and I'll catch you up. I promised to meet Iestyn and the boys by the Figure Eight, so I'll see you back on the train."

"Don't you get lost, our Billy," said Aunty Scissors Ann.

"Mam, I'm sixteen!" said Billy indignantly.

His mother sniffed, and followed us to the Fair. It was lovely, noisy and crowded, and there was lights and loud music, and I had Candy Floss and two rides on the big horses and one ride on a huge cockerel, and Dadda won a coconut for me - a real coconut. At last it was time to go to the station. By now the story of my escapade was being spread around the people from our Chapel.

"Lost all day she was!"

"'Only found her two minutes before they left the beach.''

"Poor little soul, looks proper poorly, don't she?" (Nanci Powell and Gwyneth were with their parents and they looked at me all admiring. I had been lost and was found. That beat yellow frills any day, I thought.)

As the train came in, I found Siencyn Oddjobs beside me. Breathing Extra Strong Mints at me, he whispered, "Your share," and pushed thrupence into my hand. 'My share of what?' I thought, but then we were pushing and shoving to get into the train. I got the corner seat again.

"Where's Siencyn?" asked Dadda.

"Don't mention that name to me," said Mam. "Losing Megan like that." But Dadda was leaning out of the window, waving and shouting, "Come on, Siencyn, room for one more."

Sheepishly, Siencyn got into the compartment, and sat by Billy. As he passed Mam and Aunty Scissors Ann they got a whiff of the Extra Strong Mints.

Aunty Scissors Ann looked at Mam. "You know where he've been," she whispered, tight-lipped.

"Not on a Sunday School Outing, surely!" said Mam. They stared at Siencyn. He blinked guiltily, and stared out of the window.

"Shouldn't be allowed," said Aunty Scissors Ann.

The Guard blew his whistle and the green flag was waved and slowly the big iron wheels turned and we were off.

"What a day!" said Mam. "Worn out, I am. Anybody want a Welsh cake?"

I sat leaning against the comfort of my father's arm. I was tired, but full of content. I was with my family. I had had rides at the Fair and my coconut was in Dadda's fish frail. In my pocket was the threepence Siencyn had given me - six whole happoths of dolly mixtures and jubes and mint Imperials and pear drops and coconut mushrooms and Tiger Nuts.

The train gently rocked us as we went on our way home, and the dusk deepened. Voices became further and further away as I leaned more heavily against Dadda, and my eyelids became more and more heavy, and with a sigh, I fell fast asleep.

CHAPTER 13

X-RAY EYES

We were playing shop outside Siân's house when Violet Pugh came and sat on the Bailey wall. She was sucking Bull's Eyes, and kept taking them out of her mouth to see how the colour had changed.

"What are you playing?" she asked.

"Shop," we told her.

"Playing shops is kid's games." Violet Pugh was in Standard V.

We went on setting out our dolls' plates with leaves and grasses for vegetables and jam jars full of stones and bits of broken twigs for sweets.

Violet Pugh went on sucking her Bull's Eyes, one in each cheek. Suddenly she said, "See that man over there?"

We looked; it was Mr Hughes Top House's lodger, old William Williams Willoughby. He shuffled slowly past us, greasy grey cap, greasy grey hair hanging over his ears, and a dirty overcoat, stained and tattered, almost reaching his cracked boots.

"He have got X-ray eyes," she went on. "He can see round corners and through walls. He can see you in the bath!"

Siân and I looked at each other in horror. "He can't, can he?" I asked.

"Yes," she said. "X-ray eyes he do have."

She got off the Bailey wall and went off, leaving Siân and me feeling very disquieted.

"It's Friday today!" I said. "Bath night."

"I know," said Siân miserably. "Well I'm not going to have a bath tonight."

"Me neither," I said. "I don't want no William Williams Willoughby seeing me in the bath."

It was no good, of course. When I got home, the bucket of water was boiling on the fire, and my clean pyjamas warming on the oven door. The tin bath was on the mat in front of the fire.

"Get undressed now," said Mam. "And keep back while I pour the hot water in."

"I don't think I want a bath tonight," I said.

"Why ever not?" asked Mam. "Come on now, no old nonsense."

"I can't," I said. "Because of William Williams Willoughby."

"In the name of faith," said Mam. "What has old William Williams Willoughby got to do with you having a bath?"

"He can see me in the bath," I told her. "He've got X-ray eyes."

"Well I've heard everything now. X-ray eyes indeed. There's no such thing as X-ray eyes. Into the bath with you now."

There was quite a struggle and a smacked bottom before I gave in. And I sat in the bath with my knees up under my chin, feeling those awful eyes peering at me through three houses, around the furniture, and under the stairs, till they got to me. I didn't breath properly till I was in my pyjamas and Mam was drying my hair.

That night, I suddenly realised, that William Williams Willoughby could see me in bed. I pulled the bed clothes up to my chin, and was a long time before I got to sleep. Even then, I dreamed of staring eyes and tin baths.

The next day being Saturday, Siân called for me to go and spend out ha'penny pocket money. As we went along the street to the sweet shop, I suddenly asked her, "Who do you believe most, your mother and my mother and all the world - or Violet Pugh?"

Without any hesitation, Siân said, "Violet Pugh."

"Me too," I said. It was all very well for Mam to say there's no such thing as X-ray eyes. Violet Pugh knew better.

I was so miserable, even coconut mushrooms couldn't console me.

That afternoon me and Dadda went for a walk while Mam went to Ponty Market. It was good to get away from the valley, to climb up over the mountain, to the sheep, and the streams and feel the clean wind singing in our ears. On the way back, we just happened to call in at Siencyn Oddjob's shack.

"*Swmai*," he called. "Come you in." And we sat in the smoky, dusty room, and he and Dadda lit their pipes and smoked, and Dadda found he'd got a bag of losins in his pocket which he gave me to keep me quiet. The glass in the case the fox was in had been smashed ages ago when one of the chickens knocked it off the shelf, so Siencyn had taken the rest of the glass out, and he used to let me play with it. I used to brush the fox with Siencyn's hair brush, and clean it's teeth with my hankie. Mam never knew of course. We just never got round to mentioning our visits to Siencyn to her.

"Look at that by there," Siencyn was saying. "Ever see such a big wart? Big as a gumboil, that is. I tried all ways to get rid of it, but no go. Had one when I was living in Somerset I did, and an old woman got rid of it for me. Said a charm, she did, and I go to sea, there it was gone. Cost me sixpence, but sixpence well spent.

"That old woman knew charms and spells for all sorts. Anyone in trouble went to her, and she said charms, and things, and she always turned up trumps. Proper wise woman, she was."

"You don't want to believe in that old rubbish," said Dadda. "Your wart will go when it's good and ready. Had one myself once, and it went by itself. Charms and spells indeed."

"You can laugh," said Oddjobs. "But I know, what I know. Pity I didn't know someone round here could do a bit of wart charming. I'll find out, don't you fret."

Siencyn's words kept running through my head all the way home. 'Anyone in trouble went to her.' 'That old woman knew charms and spells for all sorts.' I wished I knew a wise woman who could help me!

I was in trouble with William Williams Willoughby's eyes. If only I knew who could help me.

And then after tea, when I took my ball out to play, there was Violet Pugh sitting on Siân's Bailey wall

"'Ullo," she said to me.

"Do you know a wise woman what does spells and charms?" I asked her.

Violet Pugh looked cunning.

"I might," she said. "What you want a wise woman for?"

"I want to make William Williams Willoughby's eyes stop being X-ray," I said

"Oh that!" said Violet Pugh. "Funny you should ask me, but I know a spell to get rid of X-ray eyes. My Auntie Aggie's a good one to do spells, and she showed me."

"Could you do a spell for me?" I begged.

"I might," she said.

"Oh, Please," I said. "I don't want nobody to see me in the bath."

"Well then," said Violet Pugh, getting off the Bailey wall. "I could do a spell for you. I don't know if it will work, like, some spells do and some don't. But the best spells work if you've got a bit of silver."

I felt disappointed. "I haven't got no silver," I said. "We don't have silver things in our house."

"Money is silver," said Violet Pugh. "A threepenny bit is silver."

"I got one in my money box," I told her excitedly.

"Well you go and get it, and I'll get the other magic things, and meet me here now just."

I was going to commit a terrible crime - taking threepence out of my money box without asking Mam. I knew she'd say 'no', and I felt too desperate to worry about the consequences when Mam found out.

I crept into the house. Dadda was out the back talking to Mr Phillips over the wall about the best way to grow rhubarb, and Mam was out - probably down Aunty Scissors Ann's. I sneaked into the kitchen and took a knife from the drawer, then got a chair and reached my money box from the mantelpiece in the middle room. I put the knife in the slot, and out came a penny, a ha'penny, another penny, two ha'pennies, another penny - where oh where was my threepenny bit? - another penny, then joy! There it was!

I put the money back and put the box back on the mantelpiece, put the chair and the knife away and rushed back to meet Violet Pugh. What if she wasn't there? But no! It was all right. She was waiting for me.

"I got the things," she said. "You got the silver?"

I showed her my threepenny bit.

"Good," she said. "Come on, we got to go by my back lane gate. There's the best place."

I followed her round the corner. Outside her gate she squatted down, and made a hole in the earth with a stick.

"Now," she said. "Put the silver in the hole."

I did so. Then she put a piece of silver paper over it, and a piece of a broken old blue iodine bottle over the silver paper, and covered it all with earth.

"Now," she said. "I got to say the spell, but you mustn't listen. Put your hands over your ears." I did so. I saw her lips move as she said the spell - I was beginning to feel a bit frightened. I wondered if Violet Pugh was a Witch. I wouldn't have put it past her.

She stood up. I got up too, and took my hands away from my ears.

"What next?" I asked.

"Well you got to run to the school wall, tap it three times, and come back. If the silver is gone, the spell's worked. I'm going home now, so long."

She opened her gate and went in. I set off, running down the street, down the school lane, tapped the wall three times and ran back. By the time I got back to Violet Pugh's back gate, I was out of breath, but I picked up the stick and began to move the earth over the place where the silver was hidden. I was so afraid, I could hardly breathe. There was the blue glass of the old iodine bottle - there was the silver paper, then Oh! Joy! The silver was gone! The spell had worked. I felt so happy, so proud! I'd saved the modesty of all the women and girls in the whole place. I was a heroine, little Joan of Arc, or Florence Nightingale. I walked away like the way I'd seen heroines doing it in the pictures, head up, smiling a little, proud but modest. I walked this way out of the back lane, round the corner, along past Siân's house. I was so busy being a heroine I didn't look where I was going. I bumped into somebody, into somebody's dirty mac above cracked and sloppy shoes. I looked up into the face of William Williams Willoughby and screamed! His eyes! The spell had worked too well! His eyes! He had two glass eggs with black staring lumps in the middle where his eyes should have been, The spell had gone wrong! I burst into tears and ran home.

Sobbing and out of breath, I raced into the house and flung myself at Dadda as he sat by the table reading the paper.

"What's the matter, *merch i*?" said Dadda, but I could only sob and sob, and the words wouldn't come out.

"What's all this?" said Mam, coming in from the middle room, with a colander of shelled peas in her hand. "Stop that noise at once, or I'll smack your bottom!"

Hiccupping and sobbing, gradually I quietened down. "Now," said Mam. "Tell me what's the matter."

So I did, I told her the whole story, the spell and the silver, and Violet Pugh, and Siencyn Oddjobs and warts and wise women and X-ray eyes and glass eggs, until at last the whole story was out.

"Well," said Mam. "I've never in all my born days heard such rubbish! Violet Pugh's spending your threepence at the chip shop this very minute, if I know anything of the Pughs, and her thinking you're the biggest *dwp* this side of Ponty. And stealing out of your money box! And listening to that old flag Siencyn - you deserve a good smacked bottom and bed!"

I burst out crying again, but Dadda took out his hankie and wiped my eyes and said, "There, there, it's all right. William Williams Willoughby hasn't got glass eggs for eyes - it's his new glasses - near blind he is, poor old dab - couldn't see two yards in front of his hand let alone through walls and round corners. His brother in Slough is doing well on the buses, good little job he've got, and he sent money for Mrs Hughes Top House to make sure his brother bought real good glasses. That's all it was, just him wearing thick glasses, and his eyes being magnified like behind them thick lenses."

"You sure?" I asked tearfully.

"Positive," said Dadda. "Don't cry, there's a good girl."

Mam looked at me, pointed to the door and said, "Bed. At once. And no supper."

I got off Dadda's lap and snivelled my way upstairs. I got into bed. Other children were out in the street, playing until proper bed time.

'That's what you get for trying to save people,' I thought.

I could hear Mam and Dad's voices downstairs, and Dadda laughing, then Mam going out of the front door.

"I'll take these cakes to Cissie Ann," I heard her say, and the front door banged.

Ten minutes later I heard Dadda coming upstairs.

"All right now?" he asked. "Come on, here's some bread and milk. Mam have cooled down a bit, and said you can have supper, and she've put a lovely bit of butter on the top."

I sat up in bed, and was soon enjoying the warm sweet bread and milk.

"Shall I read you a story?" asked Dadda. "What'll it be? He looked at books on the shelf by the bed. "*Grimm's Fairy Tales, Hansel and Gretel, The Frog Prince?*"

"No thanks," I said. "I've had enough magic spells and witches for one day. If you don't mind, I think you'd better make it *Winnie the Pooh*."

CHAPTER 14

THE DIAMOND JUBILEE

"Big Meetings on Sunday," said Mam. "We'll have to go to Ponty on Saturday to get you a new outfit."

It was always the same. Something nice happened, but there was always a snag. I wanted to have a new outfit - Mary Rees had a new coat with a real fur collar - but I didn't want to go to Big Meetings. I didn't know why the grown up people had to have them. The prayers went on and on, and the sermon lasted for even longer than usual. I liked the singing though. That was the best part, but we always had to go early to Big Meetings, because the Chapel was full half an hour before the service began. The whole thing used to last forever.

And then I found out that this year's Big Meetings was special. Dadda and I had called in to see Siencyn Oddjobs, and we were sitting by the fire, nice and cwtchy, I was eating a ha'porth of Marshmallows that Dadda had bought for me in Miss Hughes - Evans' shop, and he and Siencyn were smoking their pipes.

"Big Meetings Sunday," said Dadda. "We got the Reverend Mafeking Williams coming - Big Preacher, by what I hear, and been to college."

Siencyn spat on the fire. He was still not used to being stopped from spitting by Marged, and his aim was still hit and miss.

"Can't stand Chapel," he said. "Haven't been for years. Marged goes to

Soar now, I heard. Gone all religious, they tell me."

"It would do you good to come," said Dadda. "Nothing like a good sermon to start the week. And William Lewis Amen is going to pray in the morning and the night as well. It's his Diamond Jubilee."

"Jawch, what's that?" said Siencyn.

I was interested too, I knew what diamonds were - Kings and Queens had them in their crowns, and on chains round their necks. I wondered if William Lewis Amen would be covered with diamonds like that, standing all glittering in the Big Seat.

"It's like Queen Victoria and her Diamond Jubilee," Dadda told us. "She was Queen for sixty years, so there's going to be a bit of a fuss for him. He's praying on Sunday and there's going to be a tea for him on Monday night, in the vestry."

I was disappointed - no diamonds - but at least there would be a Chapel tea, with salmon sandwiches and slab cake.

"He's a good man," said Oddjobs. "He's a regular Christian, and if there's a heaven, he'll have the front seat."

He made Heaven sound like a Chapel. Perhaps Heaven was just Big Meetings up in the sky. It was all very depressing.

"I wouldn't mind going to hear him pray," said Siencyn as we left. "I got a suit I can wear, and there's a clean shirt somewhere."

"It says on the notices 'All Welcome'," I said.

"It always does," he replied.

I liked William Lewis Amen - all of us children did. Although he was a Chapel Deacon, we weren't shy of him. He was a small quiet man, with white hair and a short white beard, and blue eyes that looked all water

He always had a few dolly mixtures in his waistcoat pocket and he used to give them to us and tell us to be good children. There was another reason, we liked him; when he got up to pray, he stood facing us all, just at the end of the row of Big Seats, where the spare hymn books were ready in case anybody wanted one. He would take one in his hands, and then tell God the news, and say thank you to Him, or tell God how lovely His earth looked in the autumn weather and suddenly he would shout Hallelujah! and the hymn book would sail through the air. Usually somebody near the front caught it, because he couldn't throw very far. Then he would grope with his eyes shut for the next hymn book, and we would peep through our fingers to see how long it would be before that went flying out of his hands as well. Big Meetings began to look more interesting.

Then when we got home, Aunty Scissors Ann was there. She was looking more snappy than usual.

"Go and wash your hands and come up to the table," said Mam. "Tea's wet, and there's a nice brown egg for you."

Aunty Scissors Ann sniffed. "You spoil that child," she said, and then to Dadda, who was hanging his cap behind the back door, "I just been telling Bethan that Billy's bringing a young lady home - from Cardiff, if you please. Coming to meet me she is, and thought she'd like to go to Chapel to the Big Meetings. You know what that means, don't you? Trapped my boy she has, with her posh ways and posh talk. I wouldn't be surprised if she was Church as well."

Dadda sat the table and started his tea. "Billy's old enough to go spooning," he said. "And you can't tell him who to pick and choose, not at his age, and earning a tidy wage like he is. You'll have to lose him sometime, Cissie."

"Well," said Aunty Scissors Ann. "There's a nice thing to say, and Iestyn gone these ten years. Sneaking off to see her in Cardiff on Saturdays, telling *me* he's gone to the Arms Park to see some decent Rugby, that's what Billy's been doing. And now bringing her home on Saturday, and expecting me to put out the flags."

"Where's she going to sleep?" asked Dadda.

"She's got an Aunty in Telelkebir Road. It would be up there with the crachach, wouldn't it? She's going to have breakfast there Sunday, and have dinner with me, and tea and supper too no doubt. It's all very well to put upon somebody at a minute's notice, isn't it?"

Mam cut my bread and butter into fingers for me to dip in my egg, and said, "She can have tea and supper here with us. We'll meet her on Sunday morning in Chapel anyway. She's probably a nice girl, homely like one of us."

"No she's not," said Aunty Scissors Ann. "A floor walker in a big shop, where all the rich ladies buy their frocks, that's what she is. All toffee nosed and stuck up. I could give our Billy what for."

Big Meetings seemed to be getting better all the time! A new outfit, William Lewis Amen's diamonds and a visitor from Cardiff and all on the same day!

Mam bought me a nice new coat called crushed strawberry colour, and a brown felt hat with a ribbon. She put my hair in rags on Saturday night, so that I had a headache and corkscrew curls on Sunday morning. We got to Chapel early, but already the people were there in crowds. The Deacons were showing people where to sit, and giving out hymn books and looking important. We sat by the front, so I had to look round to see if Mary Rees was wearing her new coat - she was, and I didn't think much of it. Time went by slowly, the Chapel got full, and the organist began to play, and still it wasn't time to begin. I heard Mam say, under her breath to Dadda, "Look who's come in!" I peeped round. It was Siencyn! Siencyn Oddjobs, in a suit, bright rust coloured, tough tweed it was and a collar coming up to his ears. Siencyn Oddjobs in Chapel!

"Well," said Mam. "Now I've seen everything!"

He must have had new boots too, because as he walked down the aisle they squeaked ever so loud. One of the Deacons showed him an empty seat by Mrs Price Richards Milk - she gave him a look, but Siencyn didn't bother. I tried to wave to him, but Mam stopped me.

Then, "There's Billy and his young lady," whispered Dadda. "Up there, second row in the gallery."

I looked up - Billy smiled at me, and whispered to the young lady. She looked down at me, and I knew I didn't like her at all. She was very smart, I could see that, all in blue, with a perm and pearl earrings, but her face was as sharp as Aunty Scissors Ann's. She didn't smile at me - just looked and turned her head away, and pretended to be looking in her hymn book.

Mam and Dadda looked at each other, and Mam's mouth went thin. I knew what that meant - she didn't like the looks of her either. But then the Preacher came in, and the service started.

The Reverend Mafeking Williams was tall and thin, with a high shiny collar and small glasses that pinched his nose. I felt a bit afraid of him - he had a look that went right through me, as if he knew all about the times when I hadn't been good. I pulled my hat down over my eyes, so he couldn't see me.

We had a hymn, and then a prayer, and a hymn again and readings from the Bible, and then William Lewis Amen got up to pray.

'This is it,' I thought, and pushed my hat back up to watch.

He turned round to us and said, "Let us go together to the Mercy Seat," and picked up a hymn book from the pile on the end of the railing round the Deacon's Big Seats. He closed his eyes, and held the book in front of him in his two hands, and started to talk to God. He said, 'Thank you' to Him for letting him be a Christian for sixty years, and for all His Goodness in keeping a wayward lad from sin. He went on like that for a little bit, then getting the hwyl, he shouted "Glory Be" and flung out his arms. The hymn book sailed through the air, and a man in one of the side pews caught it.

"Amen," said the congregation.

"And Thank You for our lovely Chapel, and all the good people gathered here to hear Thy Words to-day," he went on. And then an amazing thing happened, Mr W R Morgan, the Headmaster of the Boys School and one of the Deacons, got up, and picked up the pile of hymn books and put them on the table by the Bible.

There was a gasp all-round the Chapel - shows how many people didn't have their eyes shut, I thought. William Lewis stretched out his hand for another hymn book, he felt where it ought to have been, and there wasn't nothing there. He opened his eyes, they looked all puzzled. He closed them again, but he didn't pray much after that. It was as if he couldn't think what to say. Mam was looking daggers at Mr Morgan, and her face was red.

The sermon was very long, and all about sin, so I thought about something else instead.

I didn't see Oddjobs to talk to when we came out of Chapel. But we met Billy and his young lady. She talked very posh, just like Aunty Scissors Ann said she would. We didn't stay with them long because Aunty Scissors Ann was cooking dinner and they had to get back.

As they went off, Dadda said to Mam, "Poor Billy's gone out of the frying pan into the fire. That girl's as bad as his mother."

When we got home, we all went upstairs to change out of our best. I could hear Mam talking to Dadda in their bedroom. "I could have wrung that man's neck," said Mam. "What right did he have to upset an old man like that. Poor old dab, he was put right off his stroke. I've never heard him pray so poor. He always prays beautiful, and today of all days, for this to have happened! W R Morgan is too big for his boots."

It wasn't a very nice day, I thought. Nobody seemed happy, except Billy. When I came home from afternoon Sunday School, he and the young lady were there. She was sitting on the sofa by him.

"Hello *merch i*," he said. "Come and sit by here, and get to know Cynthia. There's plenty of room for a little *dwt* like you."

"Do be careful of my dress," said the young lady. "You are creasing it, wriggling about like that."

"Tea's ready," said Mam, so we all sat round the table.

It was a lovely tea, with sandwiches, and trifle and cake and apple tart.

"Pass round the salmon sandwiches," said Mam to Dadda, "While I pour the tea."

"Not for me, thank you," said Cynthia. "May I be an awful nuisance and have just plain bread and butter?"

Mam put the tea down with a thump and went into the back kitchen to get it. Cynthia said something about there being no serviettes and put her handkerchief on her lap.

"What did you think of the service?" Dadda asked her.

"Very interesting," she replied. "Of course, I'm not Chapel, so it was all very new to me. Rather blood and thunder I thought. Gorgeous singing of course, and that poor quaint old man throwing that book! I thought I'd die trying not to laugh."

Mam was sawing through the loaf as if it was somebody's neck.

"He's a lovely man," said Mam. "And a thorough Christian. He do always pray beautiful. We do understand him in our Chapel, not outsiders."

"Ah well," giggled Cynthia. "Perhaps he'll do better this evening. After all, he's not trained in that sort of thing."

"You don't have to go to College to talk to your Maker," snapped Mam.

"Have some trifle," said Dadda, but Cynthia wouldn't. I was glad the tea was over.

The Chapel was packed again that night. It was so full, some of the men were sitting on the window sills. We were in our usual place near the front, and Billy and Cynthia and Aunty Scissors Ann were up in the gallery. Dadda used to say that Aunty Scissors Ann always went up there because she could see better what everybody was up to.

The singing was lovely. The hymns went up, up, right through the Chapel roof to the sky. And the William Lewis Amen stood up to pray. He looked very small and old, and sad. He didn't seem to be enjoying his jubilee at all.

"Dear friends, let us approach God's Throne in prayer," he said and closed his eyes. There were no books in front of him. There was a silence, all over the Chapel; it was as if no-one breathed. And then we heard, 'Squeak, squeak, squeak, thump!' The noise seemed to be coming down the aisle.

I peeped round - it was Oddjobs, Siencyn Oddjobs was coming down the aisle on tip toes in his new boots, collecting hymn books from in front of people who were sitting with their hands covering their eyes, ready to pray. As he came his pile grew bigger. When he came to the Big Seats, he quietly put the books on the flat top of the rail in front of William Lewis Amen. The Reverend Mafeking Williams looked down at Siencyn, and Siencyn looked up at the Reverend Mafeking Williams. The Chapel was hushed. Then the Minister put his hands over his eyes and bent his head, and Oddjobs squeaked and thumped back to his seat.

William Lewis felt in front of him, his hand touched a book, he picked it up, and the congregation sighed like a big whisper all-round the Chapel.

Oh, how he prayed! He Thanked God for all His Goodness, for the sky and the stars and the lovely sun, for the mountains, and the view from the top of Pen-y-waun, which was a real treat.

"Bountiful are Thy Works, Oh Lord," he cried. "Allelulia," and the hymn book went up in the air and Mrs Price Richards Milk caught it. He felt for another hymn book, found it, and Thanked God for all the little children in the Chapel, and for Mrs Jones, Five Tymawr Terrace's safe delivery. "A lovely boy, Oh Lord, but we were all worried for a bit." He reminded God that Franklyn Jones had broken his leg, last Tuesday on the day shift, and was much better, but Granny Pugh's cough was worse. He asked God to Bless all those who worked underground, digging like moles through the bowels of the earth, and to help all the men on the dole to keep their Faith and their Hope, to give Peace to the Troubled, and Salvation to the Sinner. "Oh Lord," he cried. "Your Loving Salvation is Everywhere, Allelulia!" And this time Dadda caught the hymn book. I felt so proud!

"Oh Lord," said the old man, as he grasped another book. "For sixty years I've loved You, and grown old in Your Service. You sustained me with Your Loving Arms when my dear wife went up to Heaven, and before that, when You took, in your Love and Wisdom, our little child. I know there's a place for me by your side, and I'm ready to come when you want me. 'Thy will be done', but I'm getting very tired."

And then, in a sweet, shaky voice he began to sing 'Praise God from whom all Blessings flow' - some of the people began to join in, then the organist played, until, by the time we came to 'Praise Father, Son and Holy Ghost,' the whole Chapel was song.

When the hymn was finished, we sang it again. Then William Lewis said, "Amen, Amen, Amen." He opened his blue, blue eyes, and smiled, then sat down.

Mam was wiping her eyes with her hankie, and a lot of men were blowing their noses. The next hymn was one of my favourites, all about a Diadem. "Crown Him," sang the Sopranos and altos. "Crown Him," replied the tenors and basses. "Crown Him and Crow-ow-own Him Lord of All," we all sang.

The sermon lasted a long time, and the Reverend Mafeking Williams went on about sin and hell a lot, but I didn't mind. Mam gave me a big humbug to suck - she'd never ever given me a sweet in Chapel before. It was a big one, and I sucked my way through the sermon.

When it was all over, and we were outside the Chapel, Mam collard Siencyn.

"How are you Mr Jenkins?" she said. "Lovely Service."

Siencyn blushed as red as his suit. "Aye, indeed," he said. "Lovely."

"I wonder if you'd like to come home with us and have a bit of supper?" said Mam.

"O darrow," said Siencyn in surprise.

Mam was even smiling at him!

"Come on," said Dadda. "You don't get an invite like that every day of the week," and he took my hand and off we all went, Mam smiling all over her face, Oddjobs looking nervous, and Billy and Cynthia walking behind.

"Come you in," said Mam. "And sit you down. The kettle won't take long." Oddjobs sat on the edge of his chair, hardly believing his luck. As Mam fussed about laying the table and making tea, she was singing to herself all the time.

It was a lovely supper, cold meat left over from dinner, and fried-up potatoes and cabbage. Then there was trifle and cake and apple tart and a nice cup of tea. Mam piled Oddjobs' plate up with food.

"Eat you up, Mr Jenkins," she said. "Plenty more if you want it."

"What about you, Cynthia? Bread and butter, is it?"

Dadda tipped his tea on the best cloth. "Never mind," said Mam. "Accidents will happen."

Dadda and I looked at each other. What was the matter with Mam?

We had nearly finished supper, when our next door neighbour, Mrs Prosser, came in. She couldn't go to Chapel because old Granny Prosser was ninety-six and couldn't be left by herself.

"Have a cup in hand?" asked Mam.

"Well I don't say no," Mrs Prosser said. She looked very surprised to see Oddjobs sitting at the table with us, crumbs on his suit and trifle on his chin.

Mam introduced her to Cynthia, who was looking as if she'd swallowed a prune.

"I really came in to see how the Big Meetings went." Mrs Prosser slurped her tea, Oddjobs poured his into his saucer, and blew on it and swilled it down. Cynthia looked shocked.

"I'll tell you how the Big Meetings went," said Mam. "The Preacher was pretty powerful - bit slow starting, but a lot of *hwyl* at the end. You could hear him in Tonypandy, I reckon.

As for the singing, well a good organist and full Chapel will raise the roof any day. But the best of all was William Lewis Amen. What a jubilee he had!"

Mam looked at Cynthia. I think 'Triumphant' is the word you'd use for the way she looked.

"William Lewis Amen prayed, and he prayed beautiful."

CHAPTER 15

THE LITTLE SAINT

We was going back to school one afternoon when Violet Pugh called out to me, "Your friend Siân's got chicken pox."

"I didn't know," I said. "What's chicken pox?"

"It's when you get chickies running all over you," Violet Pugh was chewing bubbly gum, and she blew a big bubble. It went 'Pop' and she sucked it all back in and went on chewing.

"And you know what chickens have got, don't you? FLEAS! She've got them all over her too."

I was frightened for Siân. Violet Pugh knew everything, and I didn't doubt for one minute that she was right. After all she was in Standard VI. My only consolation was that I was sure Siân's mother would be able to cope with the chickens and the fleas too. Two days later, I showed Mam some itchy spots on my leg and before long Dr Evans was telling me that I had the chicken pox too. I burst into tears and asked if the chickens was coming soon, and Mam and Dr Evans found out all about Violet Pugh and what she had told me, and they had a good laugh.

I didn't like having them spots, but that was better than what I was expecting, and Mam made me egg custards, and Siencyn gave Dadda a peach to give to me and the Sunday School sent grapes – GRAPES! Perhaps I was more ill than I thought! My Sunday School teacher came, and gave me a book and told me to be a good girl, and cousin Billy brought me a bottle of pop. Auntie Scissors Anne came to see me and looked pleased that I looked so spotty.

"Well, you *are* a fine picture, I must say," she sniffed at me. "And spoilt rotten by everybody too, I've no doubt."

"She's a good little girl," said Siencyn, who had called in to give me a bag of fruit drops.

They wouldn't let me go to school for three weeks, even though I felt well and the spots was gone. I couldn't play with my friends, so they wouldn't catch it, and I had nothing much I wanted to do, so I started to read the book my Sunday School teacher brought me. It was a revelation! It was all about a girl my age called Little Posy. She lived in a big house and had nice clothes and good food, but it said, 'she sorrowed for those worse off than herself.' She read improving books to the widows and orphans, who blessed her good counsel. Then she found a beggar woman dying in the gutter, and she exhorted her to repent. She gave her best pelisse to a child who didn't have one, and who wore rags – I had to ask Mam what a pelisse was, and she had to look it up in the dictionary – it was a sort of coat - and she did all sorts of good and noble deeds. No wonder all the people called her 'The little Saint' and blessed her name and thought the world of her. I decided there and then that I would be just like Little Posy and be a little saint. I felt full of good and noble thoughts. As there was nothing else to do that afternoon, I thought I'd start straight away.

The first drawback was that there was no beggar woman dying in our gutter. Come to think about it, I don't think I ever saw one in anybody's gutter – except in Little Posy's of course. There was a lovely picture of it in the book, with Little Posy lifting her eyes to the sky. I thought I'd try the widows next, and reading improving books to them, - but I didn't know any widows or improving books. I asked Auntie Scissors Anne if she'd like me to read to her – after all she'd been a widow for years, till Uncle Iestyn turned up again from Penarth, but she told me not to be so cheeky! Being a saint like Little Posy was hard work – I hadn't even got started and I'd been at it for half an hour.

Three o'clock, and Mam said she was going next door to Mrs Pryce Thomas's to take a bit of cake for Granny Williams' tea, and be a good girl and play quiet for five minutes. I looked through the good works of Little Posy again – she was hot on exhorting people to be good. If I knew what it meant, I'd do a nit of exhorting myself too I thought.

There was a knock on the front door, I went and opened it, and there on the doorstep was a gypsy with a basket of pegs.

"Is your Mam in, my little love?" she asked.

"No," I said. "She's out. There's nobody in except me."

The gypsy looked interested. "You look as if you're a good little girl – the joy of your Mam and Dad, I can tell."

"Oh yes," I said. "I'm their joy all right."

"A good and generous little girl – give a helping hand to anybody in need, wouldn't you?"

"Oh yes," I said, feeling just like Little Posy.

"I got a little girl your age. Poor child, she haven't got nice clothes like you. Freezes to death every winter, she do!"

"Oh dear," I said. "There's sad."

"Pity you haven't got a coat you could spare, isn't it? Stop her freezing to death again this winter, it would. But perhaps you haven't got no coat to spare. Your kind heart would give a coat to a poor child if you had one."

"I got my best winter coat," I said. "I don't wear it in the summer."

"There's sensible," said the gypsy. "You got it handy?"

"Yes" I said. "It's upstairs in the wardrobe." She sighed and looked sad, and her eyes were bright as buttons.

"You wait by here," I said. "I'll get it quick."

I ran upstairs. I was Little Posy giving to the poor, and being blessed by all. I got the coat down off the hanger, took the sheet off it and put the mothballs on Mam's dressing table, I ran downstairs. The gypsy was looking up and down the street, and seemed a bit worried.

"Here it is," I said.

The gypsy took it quickly – she grabbed it out of my hand.

"Lovely," she said. "I'll just run home with it and see if it fits." And she was gone! No thank you, no blessing, no looks of admiration. She was gone down the street and was out of sight, I felt disappointed. No-one treated Little Posy like that. For the first time I began to wonder about Little Posy.

There was a slam of the back garden gate and Mam rushed in. "You all right, *merch i*? I came as soon as I could. Don't you answer the door now. Sal Top House just called in to Granny Williams and said there's a gypsy in the street. Don't you be afraid of her now."

"I'm not afraid," I said. "She've been here. She's just gone."

"She won't hurt you love," said Mam.

"I know," I said. "She was a very sad, poor gypsy – got a little girl like me, she said, only not so lucky, and got no nice clothes to wear. Ever so grateful, she was."

Mam sat down suddenly. "What do you mean, grateful? You didn't give her nothing, did you?"

I smiled at Mam – wasn't she going to be pleased?

"I gave her my winter's coat," I said. "I have helped to rescue the perishing."

That did it! Mam called me a naughty girl, and a little flag, and running out to try and find the gypsy, and getting all the neighbours to look for her and Auntie Scissors Anne looking pleased and saying, "No wonder she can give good coats away – spoil her, you. Expects she can get a new coat every whip stitch. Thinks her father's made of money."

I was in trouble, in real bad trouble. Mam didn't smack me because I'd been poorly, but she was hopping mad, and I couldn't wait to tell Dadda all about it when he came home from the allotment with Siencyn and a bunch of jibbons. They looked surprised too.

"Did the gypsy threaten you? Did she make you give her your best coat?" asked Dadda.

"No," I said. "I just wanted to be a saint like Little Posy."

"Who's Little Posy?" asked Mam, all suspicious – so I told them all about the book my Sunday School Teacher had given to me, and how I wanted to be a saint like Little Posy and help the widows and the beggar women, and by the time I'd finished Mam had really got her moss off, Auntie Scissors Anne shocked, Dadda was red in the face and blowing his nose in his hankie and choking in his throat and Siencyn saying, "Got a good head on her, she have – go far she will. Reading books like that. The little saint, well, well, well."

I don't know how I'm going to get a winter coat for her," said Mam. "I don't indeed. She'll have to wear her everyday coat for school and Chapel. Shamed we'll be before the whole congregation."

But we wasn't shamed at all. Two days later here comes Siencyn with a brown paper parcel and inside it beautiful material for a winter coat for me! Lovely it was – crushed strawberry colour, Mam said it was, and lining, and cotton to sew it, and buttons and everything!

"Well," said Mam. "What can I say? You're a very lucky girl, you don't deserve it, I can tell you! Say thank you to Siencyn now." So I did, and I kissed his whiskery face, and he looked pleased.

"I'll just run up to little Miss Williams and see if she can make it up for us, and I can look in her pattern book and see what she've got," said Mam, wrapping the material up tidy again.

"Don't forget to call in on Cissie Anne's and show her," called Dadda, as Mam went out of the door.

"Oh you!" said Mam.

I took my book into the middle room to read. It was *Winnie the Pooh* - I'd gone off books about being good, they only got me into trouble. I could hear Dadda and Siencyn talking as they smoked their pipes.

"You haven't left yourself short of money now, have you?" Dadda was saying. "I can't get over your spending all that money on Megan, real kind of you it was."

"Cost the best part of thirty-five shillings," said Siencyn. "And I don't grudge it at all. That little girl of yours do give me more laughs at what she do get up to than George Robey on the wireless. Anyway it didn't cost *me* thirty-five shillings."

"You did come by it honest?" said Dadda, sounding worried.

Siencyn chuckled. "I won it on a horse! Don't usual bet on a horse – dogs is more my line, as you know, but this one I thought is a dead cert. After Megan trying so hard to be all goody-goody like that girl in the Sunday School book, when I seen the name of the horse in Billy the Bookie's paper I knew it couldn't lose. I put a whole shilling on it, and it came in at forty to one."

"Don't tell nobody for the love of John Thomas," said Dadda. "If my wife knew that that new Sunday coat of our Megan's came into this house because of gambling, the fat would be in the fire!"

"Mums the word," said Siencyn, chuckling.

"Well, go on," Dadda said. "Tell us the name of this flipping horse."

"It was Precious Posy – that's where it was," said Siencyn, and he laughed, and Dadda laughed, and said, "If that don't beat all."

And they laughed some more, but I couldn't see anything funny!

CHAPTER 16

OFF TO VENEZUELA IN THE MORNING

We was walking home from Chapel one Sunday night, me and Billy, when suddenly I asked him, "Where's your father buried?"

Cousin Billy was so surprised he nearly choked on his toffee.

"What on earth made you think of that now?" he asked.

"Well," I said. "We had a lesson in Sunday School today about visiting the widows and the fatherless, and I thought I'd visit you and your mother. Then I wondered where your father is buried."

Billy grinned. "You take the biscuit," he said. "The way your little mind do work beats me."

"Well, where is he buried?" I asked. "Your mother didn't take flowers to the cemetery to put on *his* grave on Flowering Sunday."

"You would notice that. Sharp as a knife you are. Well, if you must know, he's not buried nowhere. He was on a ship - a sailor he was - and he was shipwrecked and eaten by cannibals."

I was horrified. I'd seen it happen to missionaries in the pictures, but they were always rescued by Tarzan in the nick of time. Billy's father must have been shipwrecked in the wrong country. To be eaten by cannibals! To be boiled in a big pot while the cannibals danced round. Suddenly I was so frightened that I said, "I think I'm going to be sick!"

"No you're not," said Billy. "Come on, let's run home."

So we did, and I wasn't. But all the same, I was really scared.

When it came time to go to bed, I wouldn't let Mam leave me alone.

"Now what's the matter?" she asked. So I told her, "I'm afraid of the cannibals that ate Billy's father."

"Cannibals! Now what nonsense has Billy been filling your head with? Nobody ate Billy's father."

"Well, where is he?" I asked. "Billy said he was a sailor and got shipwrecked. Did he escape? I thought Billy's father was dead. Aunty Scissors Ann's always on about 'how many years it is since her Iestyn's been took."

Mam sighed and sat on the edge of my bed. "I'd better tell you, I suppose. Your Uncle Iestyn wasn't so much took, as he went. He was working underground - carpenter he was - and one day he came home and said he'd had enough of being like a mole in the dark all the time. Wanted the sun and the sky and the sea, he did, wanted to see China and Japan, and places like that, so he went off to get a job as a ship's carpenter. Got to Penarth, he did, and that's the last time we set eyes on him."

"Is he still alive?" I asked. "Is he still on a ship?"

"I don't know," said Mam. "I expect so. Said he wanted to see Venezuela."

The cannibals had retreated now, and in their place was excitement, and admiration for Uncle Iestyn.

"He could go to Mexico," I said. "Or Santiago, or the South Pole and see the penguins. Perhaps one day he'll come home with a trunk full of treasure. How long's he been gone?"

"Years and years," said Mam. "But Aunty Cissie Ann don't like to talk about it, so never you mention it to her - all right? Just pretend you know nothing. Now off to sleep."

I was quite happy to settle to sleep now, imagining I was on a ship myself, the wind blowing my hair, and South Sea Islands on the sky line.

I never told Billy or Aunty Scissors Ann I knew about Uncle Iestyn sailing the world like the Flying Dutchman, and life went on as usual until one day when Mam said we were in for a treat - we were going on a Mystery Trip.

It was the Rechabite's Annual Outing, and we were going to get a bus from outside the Chapel, and we wouldn't know where we were going until we got there!

I was so excited - almost as good as going to Venezuela, I thought. We set off after dinner, two bus-fulls of us, and had a lovely journey through the valley and down to the Vale, until at last we reached the seaside - PENARTH!

I'd never been to Penarth before, it was lovely, they had a pier and an esplanade, and I had ice cream, and sweets, and saw ships on the sea, coming from the docks and going all over the world.

Mam went off with the other ladies to help with the teas in one of the Chapel vestries.

Dadda and I went on the Pier and watched the sea, and suddenly I said, "Oh look Dadda - there's our Billy! Over there, on that bench."

Before Dadda could stop me, I ran up to him and shouted "Boo." He looked surprised - very surprised indeed.

"I didn't see you on the trip," I said. There was a man sitting next to Billy.

When he saw Dadda he said, "*Swmai* Gwyn."

And Dadda said, "Didn't expect to see you today."

And then Billy said, "This is Megan."

And the man said, "Looks just like her mother."

And Dadda said, "There's two busloads of us down for the afternoon - Do you know who's with us?"

The man and Billy got up quickly and said it was time to go - and they were gone!

The man turned his coat collar up and pulled his cap over his eyes and they were soon lost in the crowd.

"Who was that with Cousin Billy?" I asked.

"Someone I used to work with," said Dadda. "Oh look, there's a man catching fish over there." So we watched the man - but he didn't catch nothing and then we had a lovely tea in the Chapel Vestry, and back on the bus, and home.

"Don't you mention to Aunty Cissie Ann that you saw Billy in Penarth," said Dadda as we got into the house. "You don't want to get him into trouble, do you?"

Sometimes things just didn't seem to make sense to me. What was wrong with Penarth, I wondered.

Not long after that, another exciting thing happened. We got a letter from Auntie Bessie, my lovely plump Auntie Bessie, to say she was engaged to be married, and was coming to stay with us for the wedding!

Aunty Scissors Ann was furious. "It oughta not to be allowed," she said. "Married four times she've been, and widowed four times. That's more than enough for most women. But no! Not for your Bessie. She could teach Henry the eighth a thing or two."

"Seems this one's a nice chap," said Dadda. "Sells butter and eggs, and has a nice little business in Swansea Market."

"She always chooses a man with money," snapped Aunty Scissors Ann. "Her first was a greengrocer, then her second was in fish, and the third had the biggest milk round in Neath, if you can believe her, her fourth was in drapery. Four lots of Insurance! She ought to be ashamed of herself."

It got more exciting when Auntie Bessie arrived - the house seemed full of laughing and kissing and she smelt lovely of powder and scent. She had a lovely stretchy pink silk jumper, and pearl earrings, and shoes with high heels, and a handbag full of chocolates.

"Well," she said. "What do you think of my ring? My Mog insisted on an engagement ring, although we're getting married so soon. No sense in waiting at our age." And she laughed and giggled and went bright pink.

"We'll get married here in Soar, and have the reception in the Chapel vestry - Mog wants a real big do - it's the first time for him, so he wants a good crowd. And I'd like you, Gwyn, to give me away!"

Dadda looked ever so pleased. "I'd be proud to," he said.

After that it seemed all rush and fuss.

We went to Ponty for new clothes - Auntie Bessie was getting married in blue, with a hat with a spotted veil and pink rosebuds, and I had a new pink frock and straw hat, and Dadda had a new shirt and a special tie and Mam cleaned and pressed his best suit and brushed his bowler.

The only one who didn't seemed pleased was Aunty Scissors Ann. She had an invite to the reception, but didn't say if she was coming or not.

Me and Dadda went up to see Siencyn Oddjobs and give him his invitation to the wedding. He was as pleased as Punch.

"Haven't been to a wedding for years," he said. "Matter of fact, I think the last one I went to was one of your Bessie's too. Married the fishmonger that time, I remember, and there was a beautiful salmon in the reception. How's Vinegar Face taking it?"

"Got a smile like a pickled prune, she has," said Dadda. "If looks could kill!"

"I bet," said Siencyn, spitting into the fire. His aim was perfect now and he always missed the bars of the grate and got straight in the flames.

"There's Bessie had five men falling for her and your Cissie Ann couldn't keep her one and only."

"He's gone to Venezuela," I interrupted.

"If I was married to Cissie Ann I'd go to Venezuela too," said Siencyn.

The wedding was to be on the Saturday, and on the Thursday my new

Uncle Mog was going to arrive in his van - his very own van - with a leg of pork and a whole ham for Mam and Auntie Bessie to cook for the reception. Just after breakfast, here comes Aunty Scissors Ann, with a very funny smile on her face.

"Just to say, I'll be coming to the wedding after all, and bringing someone with me, as well as our Billy.

"Sorry I can't stop to help with the pork, but I'm off to Cardiff to buy something new for the wedding. So long." And she was off, leaving Mam and Auntie Bessie looking puzzled.

"What's she up to? When she's got that look on her face, somebody's in for it. I don't like it," said Mam. "Cissie Ann's got a mean streak, well, we'll find out sure enough, come on, let's get the beetroot on to boil."

Uncle Mog and the ham arrived just after dinner. You should have seen the size of the ham and the leg of pork! Uncle Mog's face was as pink as the pork, and he was as fat as Auntie Bessie - a bit quieter, but beaming.

He had pounds of butter in his van too, and jars of pickles and chutney, and dozens of eggs, a pint of cream, and soon the house was full of the smell of the meat roasting, and the stuffing and the crackling, and the ham boiling - it was great.

The next day Mam and Auntie Bessie made bowls of trifle, with thick cream on the top, then we all went and had our hair Marcel Waved - even me!

I felt like a princess. That night, I had to sleep wearing a pink hairnet to keep the waves in.

Next day the wedding was to be at twelve o'clock. All the members of the Sisterhood came and took the food down to the Chapel vestry. They were going to slice the meat and butter the bread and lay the tables and put out the pickles and sauces, and wait on us. I'd seen the wedding cake - it was lovely and Dadda carried that down to the vestry. You should have seen my new frock. I had a new petticoat and knickers to match as well, and white socks, and ankle strap shoes and Auntie Bessie put scent behind my ears and on my hankie.

Me and Mam went to Chapel together - Dadda was coming with Auntie Bessie in Mostyn Williams's car that did all the weddings and funerals in our village.

The Chapel was nearly full, and a lot of people waited outside, so they all saw my new hat and outfit.

We sat in the very front row, because Mam was Auntie Bessie's sister.

Everybody was dressed beautiful, and the organ was playing, and there were lovely flowers on the table.

People were looking behind to see if the bride was coming - the bridegroom was there already, looking even pinker, with a white starched collar that shone like a looking glass, and a pepper and salt trousers and black jacket, with his brother looking exactly the same beside him - like Tweedledum and Tweedledee, I thought. Then someone came in and sat behind us - I heard a stir, and a gasp all-round the Chapel - I peeped round, it was Aunty Scissors Ann in purple velvet with a real fox fur, and cousin Billy in his best suit and someone else I couldn't see, but Mam went red in the face, then white as a sheet. There was a hubbub of talk all round the Chapel - then the organ started 'Here comes the Bride' and in came Dadda and Auntie Bessie.

Oh! She did look posh, with a bouquet of red roses all spraying out all over the place - it was a lovely bouquet - big as a bush it was.

Mam was shaking and crying all through the service - then we had to go into the Minister's vestry to see them sign the register, then we all came out and cousin Billy took our photos with his Brownie Camera. In the Chapel vestry there was such a commotion, shaking hands, and kissing the bride, but there was just as big a commotion around Aunty Scissors Ann and a man in a grey suit. Mam and Dadda took me over to them.

"Well Cissie," said Mam. "You could have told us about Iestyn coming today. Gave me such a shock, it did. Oh, it's lovely to see you, Iestyn. Welcome home!" and she gave him a hug and a kiss.

Aunty Scissors Ann gave me such a sharp smile. "And this is your Uncle Iestyn, home from the sea, safe and sound, after all his adventures."

I looked at my new Uncle Iestyn. "I've seen you before!" I said. Dadda began to cough and splutter. "I've seen a picture of you with my father." Dadda breathed a sigh of relief. Uncle Iestyn kissed me - but he looked very unhappy.

"Places everyone!" said the Best Man, and we all went to sit down at the long trestle table.

"It's all right," I whispered to Dadda. "I won't tell. He's the man we saw with Billy at Penarth, isn't he?"

Dadda nodded. "I'll tell you after," he said.

The Minister said Grace, then we tucked in. You should have seen the food! Ham and pork cut thick, and all the salad and bread and butter and chutney and beetroot and pickled onions you wanted, then the trifle, then wedding cake and cups and cups of tea, and Aunty Scissors Ann taking all the limelight. I could hear her from where I sat.

"Oh yes, the adventures he's had - fill a book they could."

"Yes he went to China, and Japan, and Africa."

"No, he's not got no souvenirs. Lost everything in a terrible tycoon, he did."

Uncle Iestyn smiled when he was prodded, and ate his food in silence. Even when the Minister got up to say a few words, he went on and on about Uncle Iestyn's miraculous return from foreign parts and dreadful adventures on the billows, and only mentioned Auntie Bessie's Wedding in passing.

At last it was time for the happy pair to go off on their honeymoon. We all went into the street to throw confetti over them, and there was a lot of talking and laughing, and my new Uncle Mog gave me a little bangle for a present - for being the first niece he'd ever had, and hoped I wouldn't mind if he spoiled me. Mind! I gave him a big kiss on his pink, piggy face, and a big hug and kiss for Auntie Bessie, and then they got into the van - 'Mog Jones, Butter Merchant. New Laid Eggs a Speciality' all along the sides in letters that high.

And then they were off, and Dadda threw an old shoe after them for luck.

There was a lot of cleaning up to do. The dishes to wash, the leftover food to be taken home. Mam organising everybody and Aunty Scissors Ann still talking about Uncle Iestyn's miraculous return.

"My heart stopped - Oh the shock to my system. I'll never be the same woman again."

"No. No inkling he was safe, after all them years."

"Yes terrible frost bite he had, and sunstroke as well and sharks all over the place, following the ship for days."

"Come on, Iestyn, let's go home," said Dadda. He took my hand, and then called to Siencyn Oddjobs who was stuffing slices of ham in greaseproof paper into his coat pocket. "Coming with us?"

Siencyn, who knew a good opportunity when it was offered, said he'd come now just, and looked round for something to put pickled onions into.

We walked down the road. Then instead of going home, Dadda led the way up the side of the mountain. We walked in single file along the path until we came to a seat. "Let's sit a spell," suggested Dadda, so we did. We sat in silence, looking down on the valley. The wind sang in the long grass, and there were harebells by my feet.

Suddenly, I said, "You never went to any of those places, Uncle Iestyn, did you? Never to Africa or Japan or the North Pole."

"No," he said. "I never did. I got as far as Penarth, and I got stuck, just couldn't go on, somehow. Got a job as ship's carpenter all right, but there in the docks it was, and never went no further. I couldn't go back home, they'd all have laughed at me after saying I was off round the world. I couldn't face Cissie Ann's tongue. She didn't want me back, to make her look small. Mind you, sent her a postal order regular every week I did, and Billy came to see me."

"He never told me," I said. "He kept the secret all those years. Told me you was eaten by cannibals."

"Well," said Uncle Iestyn. "I'm back now. No choice when Cissie Ann decided, I had to come back. Worked a quick one there, she did, to get one over on Bessie - she never told me Bessie was getting married again." He gave a big sigh, and looked so sad.

"Never mind, Uncle Iestyn," I said. "One day, you'll go to all them places. You'll see. I'll come with you - just you and me. We'll go to India and China, and we'll see the penguins and the whales and the South Seas. We'll go to Venezuela!"

Uncle Iestyn smiled - Oh he looked so much like Dadda when he smiled.

"What about Valparaiso, and the Gulf of Mexico?"

"And we'll go round Cape Horn and Tiera Del Fuego."

Uncle Iestyn took my face between his hands. "Do you know something? I really believe that we'll do it - just you and me - by golly we'll do it. Yes, we will - Venezuela, Valparaiso and all the world."

"Well then," I said. "We'd better start saving up to go. Dadda, do you think I could have a rise in pocket money?"

CHAPTER 17

THE ELECTION

"Clean collar tonight, Bethan," said Dadda after tea.

"I know," said Mam. "It's ready for you. And I've brushed your coat, and put a clean hankie, with no holes in it, in your pocket."

"Where are you going, Dadda?" I asked as I got out my crayons and crayoning book and spread them on the green plush tablecloth.

"Important night tonight," he said. "Selection Committee. The Election is coming up soon and Silas Thomas is retiring."

"About time too," said Mam. "Poor old dab's knocking ninety."

"Ninety indeed," said Dadda. "He looks older than he is because he do worry. Not far short of sixty-five, according to his brother."

"What do you do at the Selection Committee?" I asked. I knew what a Selection Box was - I'd had one at Christmas, full of different kind of bars of chocolate. Perhaps all the members sat round and chose the chocolate they wanted and perhaps Dadda would bring some home for me.

"We got to choose a Candidate to stand in the Council Elections. A lot of good men have put their names forward."

"None as good as you would be," said Mam, as she helped him on with his coat.

Dadda laughed. "Oh go on with you, Tell you about it when I come back," he said.

I went on crayoning. Mam washed the dishes and got out her knitting, then Aunty Scissors Ann called in to borrow half a pound of currants, and Mrs Edwards Ty Top came in to sell tickets for the Drama and stopped to have a cup in hand to be friendly.

"I hear Evan John Jones Paris House is standing for the Liberals," said Mrs Edwards.

"A good man, but misguided," said Mam.

"He's like the rest," sniffed Aunty Scissors Ann. "You got to watch him like a hawk. A yard of knicker elastic is a yard of knicker elastic, in my opinion, not thirty-five and three quarter inches."

"I've always found him honest enough," said Mam. "And anyway, when did you ever go into his shop? Always get your sewing things in Ponty Market."

"Two years ago, I went in his shop and was cheated by that stuck-up assistant of his. Pulled the elastic to fit the measure, she did, and I told her so too. Never been in that shop since and never likely to go."

"It'll be a straight fight this time," said Mrs Edwards. "Just Labour and Liberals, no other."

Aunty Scissors Ann and Mrs Edwards had gone by the time Dadda got home.

"How did it go?" asked Mam.

Dadda sat down in his armchair and pulled his collar and tie off. "Bethan love," he said. "For pity's sake put the kettle on. I've had a time of it, and I'm fair worn out."

"Kettle's singing," said Mam. "Won't be a minute boiling. Who was selected then?"

"It was a close thing," said Dadda. "All this in confidence mind, but I tell you this, when Evan Jones was selected, his brother John made ructions, because *he* wasn't selected, and it nearly came to blows."

"You don't say. But John Jones have never bothered much with Politics," said Mam. "Evan's always been the boy - shook hands with Kier Hardy once, he did. Always active in the Party, good speaker and a clean liver. Never you mind, John Jones will soon calm down, and it'll all blow over."

"Oh no it won't," said Dadda. "John Jones said as it was only the Chairman's casting vote made Evan the winner, and the Chairman being Ned Watkins and a personal ill-wisher of his, he couldn't see why the electorate shouldn't have a proper choice - so he's standing as Independent Labour!"

"Never," cried Mam looking real surprised. "But he can't - he'll split the vote!"

"That's the trouble," said Dadda. "Split it he will. Evan Jones might have shook hands with Kier Hardy, but John Jones scored a try against England - and not at the Arms Park neither, but at Twickenham. And that try was scored in the last few minutes of the game and gave us the match. There's a lot will vote for John Jones for that try alone. Get into the House of Lords with a try like that he could. No, unless John Jones climbs down, this Election is going to be a real headache for us all."

As the quarrel between the brothers got really going and people taking sides, left right and centre, another candidate put himself up - old Mr Selwyn Morris, a Deacon from our Chapel, as a plain Independent.

"Heard the latest?" said Mam, as she dished up Dadda's dinner after the morning shift. "We got another gladiator in the arena. Selwyn the Psalms is standing for the Election." "Selwyn the Psalms! There's ridiculous," said Dadda. "He's a lovely old man, but he's even older than the retiring Councillor, and he've never made a political speech in his life. What do he know about committee work?"

Mam sat down at the table to watch Dadda eat his food. "Make himself a laughing stock he will," she said. "Seems he says he got to do it to bring peace to politics. When have there ever been any peace in politics? He says he's prayed about it and sees his path clear. Worried he've been about the bad feeling between Evan and John - don't forget he's their mother's first cousin once removed and he don't like family quarrels. Says everybody will vote for him and it will show the boys the error of their ways. Proper innocent old man he is, and he'll break his heart when he finds nobody's voted for him... I tell you what: I'm fed up with this Election all ready."

Next Saturday Dadda went up to Siencyn's shack after our walk, while Mam went to Ponty Market. First thing he said was "What do you think of the election then?"

"This'll be a hard fight to get Evan Jones elected, but the voters will back the official Labour candidate," said Dadda, trying to sound as if he believed it.

"Evan Jones is about as exciting as last week's fish. Shook hands with Kier Hardy indeed. That don't cut no ice with me. Now John Jones - there's a man for you!"

"You got to support the official Labour candidate," said Dadda, getting firmer.

"You got to support a National Hero," said Siencyn. "You was there. You saw that try at Twickenham. Lovely scissors, then a dummy, then he was off for the line like a flipping arrow. Classic, that try was, real classic. I

127

know where my vote is going. Mind you I always like a good election. Only time I ever get a ride in a car."

"What do you mean?" asked Dadda. "Not far for you to go to the school to vote."

Siencyn wheezed. That was the way he laughed. "I do go to William Williams Willoughby's - can't see much he can't, and I do go in the car with him to vote. Liberal he is, and they always have Phillips the Insurance's car."

"That's not very honest," said Dadda. "Riding in a Liberal car and voting Labour."

"They shouldn't try to bribe people with rides," said Siencyn, looking as if butter wouldn't melt in his mouth. "Once I had a ride in a Conservative car - now that *was* a car. It was for Parliament - not the Council that time, and I never new such a car. You could live in it and take lodgers. I sat right back and had the time of my life."

As we went off down the path to go home. Dadda called out, "Are you coming to help us at the Committee Rooms?"

Siencyn shouted, "Aye - send a Rolls Royce for me." And doubled up laughing.

"He's a boy," said Dadda to me as we walked past the old quarry.

It got more exciting as the election came nearer. First there was the Committee Rooms set up - the Liberals in Mrs Phillips Insurance's sitting room, the Labour in Mrs Lewis Tegfar's parlour, and the Independent Labour in Mrs Rhys Risca's front room. Mrs Phillips made the best tea, but Mrs Lewis was a dab hand at Welsh cakes, and Mrs Rhys didn't skimp on the butter for the ham sandwiches. There really wasn't much in it. Selwyn the Psalms didn't have a Committee Room - said everybody knew him and what he stood for, so he and his friends carried on as usual. He didn't have a political Meeting in the school neither, but the other candidates did. Dadda was working afternoons, and so Mam had to take me with her when she went to Evan Jones's Meeting. It was funny being in the school in the evening, and we all sat in the hall in the desks for Standard IV and V, and the speakers stood on Governesses Platform.

Evan Jones went on and on - I didn't listen - then questions was invited. One man in the back shouted, "Which is the hand that shook Keir Hardy's then?"

Evan Jones held up his right hand. "This is the hand that shook the hand of that great Labour Leader. I was only a young lad, but it was an honour I won't forget."

A lot of people clapped and said, "Hear, hear!"

Then someone else shouted, "No, and you won't let nobody else forget it neither."

A lot of people laughed and somebody else shouted "Which is the hand that held the ball when you scored a try for Wales, then?" And Evan Jones went red in the face, and some men in the back laughed in a nasty way.

"Rodneys, the lot of them," said Aunty Scissors Ann.

"Go and play your games somewhere else," shouted Evan Jones. "This is a serious Political Meeting, and nothing to do with games!"

"Rugby isn't a game," shouted a man built like a mountain. "Where's your National Pride?"

"Where's your Political Sense?" yelled Evan Jones. Then a lot of men stood up to argue and a lot of women said, "Shame! Sit down! Shouldn't be allowed," and it got very exciting, till Idwal Davies got up on the platform and started to sing 'Calon Lan', then everybody joined in, and after that we had he National Anthem with the chorus twice, so that the sopranos could go high on 'O *bydded i'r hen iaith barhau*.' and then the Meeting was over, and we all went home.

At last it was Election Day. We had a holiday from school, and we were told not to play by the school so as not to disturb the voters. We went out in the streets though wearing rosettes and crowds of us went about singing the election song:

Vote, Vote, for Evan Jo-o-ones,
Chuck the others up the pole,
If I had a penny gun
I would shoot them up the bum, and they wouldn't be a voter any more.

Johnnie Thomas had an old sweeping brush and he tied his rosette to it and pinned a leaflet with Evan Jones' photograph on it. We all got behind him, and sang and marched along until in Llewellyn Street we met Billy Phillips coming the other way with his rosette and sweeping brush and John Jones' photograph, and his army of singers.

We met in the middle of the street. "Out of the way," shouted Billy. "Let us pass."

"Booo," we all shouted. There was a bit of threatening and scuffling then. Johnny Thomas pushed Billy Phillips and Billy Phillips pushed Johnny Thomas, then a fight started. Just at that moment, down the street came Matthew Evans pulling his gambo covered with Blue rosettes, and his crowd singing, "Vote, vote, vote for E J Jo-o-ones."

Suddenly everybody was shouting and pushing, then doors opened, out rushed mothers shouting, "Get off home, you noisy lot." We got away as fast as we could. We ran down two streets away, when Johnny Thomas got us all into a tidy little group, put his rosette straight and off we went again. A gang of big boys stopped us.

"Who you voting for, then?"

"Evan Jones, the Official Labour Candidate."

"Garn, you want to vote Communist."

"Communists are violent people," said Siân. "My father said."

A big boy glared down at her.

"If it wasn't for the Communists, you wouldn't get your daily bread."

"We don't get our bread from the Communists, we get it from the *Co-op*," I said.

"Can't waste time talking to kids," said the Big Boy, pulling his cap down over his eyes. "Come on." And they walked off looking fierce like in the pictures.

It was all very exciting.

When the polls were shut, Dadda came home for his supper, because he and Mam and Billy were going to the Municipal Offices for the results. Aunty Scissors Ann was to stay and mind me.

Dadda was very worried. "The vote is proper split," he said. "Mark my words, the Liberals will win. They'll get in, and I could knock Evan and John Jones' heads together."

When Mam went to put on her hat and coat and change her shoes, I said to Dadda, "Did Siencyn have a ride in a big car?"

Dadda grinned. "Yes, a lovely black shiny car, and he've been to all the committee rooms, 'helping'," he said. "And he's had enough tea and Welsh cakes and ham sandwiches to last the rest of the week. He said there's no difference between Liberal, Labour and Independent when it comes to Welsh cakes."

He kissed me goodnight, and as soon as he and Mam had gone, I went to bed. I didn't want to stay and talk to Aunty Scissors Ann. It had been a very exciting day and I went to sleep ever so quick.

I think it must have been the letter box flap going flop, flop, flop-flop-flop as it always did when somebody shut the front door, that woke me. I lay quiet and heard the kitchen door shut. It was dark, but I could still see enough to find my way down stairs.

Mam and Dad were sitting by the table drinking tea.

"Megan *fach*," said Mam. "What you doing out of bed?"

"I woke up," I said. "Is Aunty Scissors Ann gone?"

"Ye,s just this minute. Here, put my cardigan round your shoulders, you'll catch your death."

"Who won?" I asked. I could see Dadda had taken his rosette off, and put it on the table. "Did Evan Jones win?"

"No *merch i*, he didn't," said Dadda. "Nor John Jones, nor Evan Jones neither. Don't ask me how he did it but our new Councillor is Selwyn Morris."

"Selwyn the Psalms!" I said. "Did he have lots and lots of votes?"

"It was real strange," said Dadda. "They all had pretty much the same number - had to have a recount twice, but Selwyn was just that bit ahead."

Mam dipped her biscuit in her tea and gave it to me.

"I just can't understand it," she said. "How could the old man have got so many votes?"

"I've been thinking about that, and there's two reasons: First, look at the ballet paper:

Evan Jones.
Evan John Jones.
John Jones.
Selwyn Morris.

"Three Joneses, all nearly the same Christian names. I think a lot of voters gave up trying to sort out which was Labour or Independent or Liberal, and went for the only name on that paper that wasn't a Jones!"

"Could be," said Mam. "And the other reason?"

"There's a lot of people in this auction do like old Selwyn, and by the end of the canvassing and all the fuss, most people got sick of the other three. Politicians can be a spiteful lot and they all think a lot of themselves. No, I think a lot of people thought, 'Poor dab, old Selwyn's a lovely man, and break his heart he will if nobody votes for him, so a few votes here and there to make him feel loved and wanted won't hurt nobody'."

"Oh," said Mam, pouring another cup of tea for Dadda. "That's what you think, is it?"

"Yes," said Dadda. "There's some people not a mile from where I'm sitting voted like that. Come on, own up."

"I will if you will," said Mam, and then they both began to laugh. "All right, I voted for Selwyn," said Mam.

"And I voted for Selwyn," said Dadda.

"And Megan, don't you tell nobody. It's our secret," said Mam.

"All right," I said.

"Come on," said Mam. "Back to bed. It's been a very big day for all of us, we're all wore out, and it's school for you tomorrow."

Life settled back down to normal very quickly.

John Jones turned professional, and went North to play Rugby for money. His friends wore black armbands for weeks.

Evan Jones bided his time, and when Selwyn retired from politics because he couldn't keep awake in the Council meetings, he got on to the Council easy. Evan John Jones went on serving in his shop, and Mam always watched like a hawk when his assistant measured the knicker elastic.

Life was peaceful and quiet again, which was just as well, because you can only stand so much excitement.

CHAPTER 18

A LOVELY GUY

"Clocks go back tonight," Mam said.

"Where do they go back to?" I asked.

"They don't go nowhere," said Mam. "We just move the hands back an hour. Tomorrow at this time it will be six o'clock."

"Why?" I asked.

"Because it's winter coming," said Mam. "Come on, finish your supper."

It was a Saturday evening, and we were having laverbread and fried bread and black pudding from the Farmers Market at Ponty. It was the best supper of the week, and sitting at the table, by the fire, with the curtains drawn against the night, and the gas light hissing gently, I felt warm and safe and cwtchy.

The back lane gate clicked. "Here comes trouble," said Dadda. "Cissie Ann's coming. What's she after now?"

Then back door latch clicked, and Aunty Scissors Ann came in like a cold wind.

"It's getting a real nip in the air," she said. "You look comfortable. Black pudding and laverbread is it?"

"Yes," said Dadda. "We've just finished our supper. Had yours have you?"

"Not yet," said Aunty Scissors Ann. "I've just been up to little Miss Williams' to get my new frock." She took off her coat, and put it over the back of the chair. "What do you think?"

She was wearing a nice navy blue dress, with bishop sleeves and a beige modesty vest.

"Turn round," said Mam. "Let's see the back."

Aunty Scissors Ann held out her arms and slowly turned round and round.

"Stop, or you'll make me giddy," said Dadda.

"Oh you!" said Aunty Scissors Ann. "Well what do you think?"

"Beautiful," said Mam. "It fits like a glove. "You can't beat little Miss Williams when it comes to fitting a frock. And she neatens all the seams lovely."

"Well," said Aunty Scissors Ann. "Her work might be all right. But her prices are not. She charges exorbitant, and I told her so too."

Mam said, "Well I've always found her reasonable, and she do always cut out economical."

"That's as may be," said Aunty Scissors Ann. "But when I get a new frock next Easter, I'm going to make it myself."

"You'll never get it to fit proper," said Mam. "And don't ask me to help you - last time I put up a hem for you, you said it looked a dog's hind leg!"

Aunty Scissors Ann sniffed. "Don't worry about me. I'd rather be independent. I've got Bopa Mary Jane's dressmaker's dummy put away somewhere and I'll bring it in and fit my frock on that. I might even do a bit of dressmaking myself. *That* would be one in the eye for little Miss Williams. Well, I can't stand round here all night. I promised to look in on Marged Siencyn Oddjobs to cheer her up a bit. Still dumpy she is, although, if I'd been married to him, and he left me, I'd have put out the flags to celebrate."

She put on her coat. "Goodnight then," she said, and then, "That child shouldn't have a rich supper like that before she goes to bed. She'll have chronic indigestion before she's much older."

The door latch clicked, and Aunty Scissors Ann was gone.

"Sometimes I wonder if Cissie Ann was born spiteful or had to work hard at it," said Dadda.

"Both," I think," said Mam. "Now she's gone I can put the kettle on and bring out the bread pudding."

I didn't like my Aunty Scissors Ann.

After Chapel next day cousin Billy said to Dadda, "How about me making Megan's Guy Fawkes this year?"

"All right," said Dadda. "You make the Guy, and I'll buy the fireworks. I've got quite a nice lot of old wood and stuff you can have for the bonfire, and some old sacks, and an old pair of working trousers in the shed. Good of you to offer."

"Wouldn't it be nice," I said. "If you could make a real Guy Fawkes - like in pictures in the History books."

"You want jam on it," laughed Dadda.

"No - that's a good idea," said Billy. "All the guys look the same - round heads and masks and dai caps and old clothes. I'm going to make a real brahma - and we'll put sparklers in his hat and on his hands for fingers "

"But no bangers," I said. "Please, and no jackie jumpers."

"Leave it to me," said Cousin Billy, looking noble.

Cousin Billy could do anything he wanted. He could have been king of the world if he'd wanted to.

Next Saturday, when Mam and Aunty Scissors Ann had left to go shopping, and Dadda was having five minutes in the armchair, I went to see how cousin Billy was getting on with my Guy. I opened his shed door, and he nearly jumped a mile.

"Oh, it's you," he said. "You made me jump. Thank goodness. I thought my mother had come back."

I knew why he'd jumped a mile - Siencyn Oddjobs was helping him. If Aunty Scissors Ann had known there would have been trouble! Cousin Billy was stuffing old straw and bracken into the sacks, and Siencyn was making the Guy's head out of an old cushion cover. He had tied string round two corners, and was putting a yellow mask on the front.

"Like it, carriad?" he asked.

"It don't look like a Guy Fawkes," I said. "It do look like a big mouse."

"*Darro*, she's right," said Siencyn. They tied the head on to the body, and stuffed the trousers and tied the bottoms of the legs with string.

"There!" said Billy. The Guy's head flopped down on to his chest. They tried to tighten the string on the neck, but the head flopped sideways.

"*Darro di*," said Siencyn. "Why can't it keep its head straight?"

"It needs something stiff for the neck," said cousin Billy. He looked round the shed, which was full of things that might come in handy, one day. I know this old walking stick. The handle is broke off, so it won't matter if it do go up in smoke."

Siencyn held the Guy's head and cousin Billy pushed the stick up the head and down the body.

"There," he said. "See - problem solved! The Guy rolled on its side and the head came off. Siencyn picked it up and looked at it.

"I won't let no Guy Fawkes beat me," he said.

"I got to go," I said. "Dadda wants me." I went home. For the first time in my life, I felt that cousin Billy had failed me.

As Guy Fawkes night got nearer, more children took their guys out on homemade gambos. At every street corner, "Penny for the Guy?" they asked.

"Shouldn't be allowed," said Aunty Scissors Ann. "And another thing, if I had my way, there'd be no fireworks neither. Burning money, that's what it is. Wilful waste will bring woeful want."

"Don't you enjoy the fireworks?" asked Dadda, all innocent, but Aunty Scissors Ann just sniffed.

I didn't go to see my Guy Fawkes again. Cousin Billy said, "Let it be a surprise."

Dadda bought the fireworks from Mrs Hughes News, and extra big sparklers, big rockets - and no bangers.

Billy arranged everything for Guy Fawkes Night. After tea, when it got dark, we were all invited to the shed to see the Guy, then me and Mam and Dadda could go to see Tommy Evans' bonfire in the next lane. They were doing theirs early because Mrs Evans wanted to get the children off to bed usual time, because they was only little. Then we could come back to our lane, and by then Cousin Billy would have put the Guy on the bonfire and the fireworks ready and it would be all ready for Dadda to light the match.

"You're a real showman," said Dadda. "Barnum and Bailey could learn a thing from you."

Guy Fawkes day, it was fine, and it never rained at all. Everything would be dry and ready to burn beautiful. I thought it would never get dark, but straight after tea, it was pitch black. I was so excited, I was nearly sick, but I didn't tell Mam.

We all put on our coats and hats and scarves and gloves and went round to cousin Billy's shed. Mam had tied cord round the lips of jam jars, and she had put candles inside, and they made lovely lanterns. We had one each, and cousin Billy had put more candles in the shed to see the Guy. We could see the light flickering through the shed window.

"Ready?" asked Billy.

"Yes," I said - though I didn't hold out much hope for a lovely Guy.

"Taa raa!" shouted Billy, and flung open the shed door.

I gasped. "It's beautiful!" I said. "It's just like in the History books. A real Guy Fawkes!"

The Guy was standing up straight, with a tall, crowned, wide-brimmed hat, with a feather made out of red crinkly paper. It had a ruff made out of paper doyleys, and a cloak down to its feet. Its arms were pinned on to the cloak, and it had more paper doyleys for cuffs. There were sparklers for fingers and sparklers round the hat, and the mask fane was ghastly and scary. It was the most wonderful Guy I'd ever seen in my life.

"Well done," said Dadda, "It's a flipping miracle."

"You're real clever," said Mam, I've never seen the like in all my born days."

Billy looked pleased as punch. "Like it?" he asked me.

"It's the best Guy in all the world," I said, and I burst into tears.

"Come on," said Mam. "Stop that crying, and let's go off to see the Evanses bonfire. "We'll be back on time." And she wiped my eyes and I blew my nose, and Aunty Scissors Ann came running out of the house, wrapped up like a parcel. "Wait for me, I'm ready."

"I thought you didn't like fireworks," said Dadda.

"Oh you!" she said. So we all went down the lane and passed the street and up the next lane where already Mr Evans was lighting the bonfire. A small crowd had gathered, and soon the flames took hold and the Guy caught fire, and Mr Evans lit the rockets.

"Oooh," we cried as the silver and gold stars burst over our heads. The sky was black and starless so the rockets looked even more wonderful. Mr Evans had a board propped on the wall by his coal cwtch with Catherine Wheels pinned to it. He lit them, one after the other, and they whizzed round and round, and stars flew in all directions. In the light of the bonfire we could see faces half in shadow half in gold all gazing at the flames and listening to the crackle of burning wood, and the zipp-pop of the fireworks, and the grey smoke rose up and everything looked mysterious and magic.

Suddenly Mrs Evans said, "John, isn't that my old coat on the Guy - the coat from behind the cwtch door?"

Mr Evans pretended not to hear. "Did you hear me - is that the coat I use for fetching the coal?"

Mr Evans said sheepily that it was, and Mrs Evans said, "Well -" and Aunty Scissors Ann said loudly that it was a shame to grudge an old coat for a bonfire - spoiling people's enjoyment. And Mrs Evans said, "Well I like that!"

And Dadda said it was time to go to our bonfire, and got us all off quick before Aunty Scissors Ann and Mrs Evans really got going.

There were other bonfires going great by this time - some up on the side of the mountain.

"I hope they'll mind the bracken," said Dadda. "We don't want trouble." By now the air was cloudy with smoke, but the rockets were bursting up and over the houses. As we came to our lane, we saw cousin Billy had got everything ready real posh. My Guy was standing up, and the bonfire ready all round him, and milk bottles with rockets in were on our wall ready.

"Do you know, that hat on your Guy rings a bell," said Mam.

"Come on," shouted Billy, "We're ready."

A little crowd from our street had gathered ready, so Dadda said, "All right, here goes. Stand back everybody!"

And he lit some matches and threw them on the bracken and the wood. Nothing happened, then a small puff of smoke, seen quite clear in the light of our lanterns, got bigger and bigger, then spread, and then it was all lit, and the flames were dancing up all red and yellow, and we could see everybody's face quite clear. I saw Siencyn Oddjobs at the back, but I thought it best to say nothing.

Billy lit the Roman Candles and Vesuvius and Golden Rain, and we all lit sparklers and waved them like magic wands. The Catherine Wheels went round with a fizz and a whoosh, and we laughed and cheered and it was wonderful.

The fire got to the Guy, and soon he was a mass of flames, and the sparklers in his hat and his fingers was sending out little stars all over the place. His arms burned and fell off, and his cloak. Then we saw what was underneath.

"My dummy!" screamed Aunty Scissors Ann. "You got my dummy!"

Bopa Mary Jones' dressmaker's dummy was well alight. 'That's why my Guy stood up so good,' I thought.

"Bit old for a dummy, aren't you?" shouted a man from Thompson Street.

Mrs Evans' best friend, Mrs Edwards Daps, who had been at Tommy's bonfire shouted, "Shame to grudge an old dummy for a bonfire - spoiling people's enjoyment." And everyone laughed.

Aunty Scissors Ann was shouting back, when Billy set the rockets off and everybody said "Ahh." So no-one could hear her, so she opened her back gate and slammed it behind her.

"Hooray," shouted someone.

"I'd better go and calm her down," said Mam, so off she went. Soon as she'd gone, Siencyn Oddjobs came and stood by us.

"Well, what do you think of your Guy?" he asked me.

"Lovely, lovely," I shouted, and Billy stoked the fire, and somebody else came down the lane with more fireworks and I held Dadda's hand and felt so happy I could fly.

At last, the bonfire died down. The fireworks was all gone. Everybody went home, or went looking for another bonfire. Dadda and Siencyn and Billy made sure the fire was all out, and safe.

"Well, I did enjoy that," said Siencyn. "I'm off now, so long."

"Going for a pint?" asked Billy.

"Pint, nothing," said Siencyn. "Tonight is special. Saved up I have, and tonight I've got enough for a double whiskey!"

"He's a lad," said Dadda, as we watched him walking away into the foggy smoke.

"Well, come on, hot supper tonight," Mam told us. So we went home.

Mam had a lovely hot stew ready for us, and bread with crispy crusts, and cousin Billy and Dadda and me washed our sooty hands and we all sat down to eat.

We could still hear bangs and noises, but they were further away now, and our kitchen fire was bright, and our supper hot and we were warm and dry and happy.

After supper, Mam made us cups of cocoa, all milk and lots of sugar.

"Is my mother still mad about that dressmaker's dummy?" asked cousin Billy.

"She's still got her moss off," said Mam. "But she's calming down. Whatever made you do it?"

"Her fault," said cousin Billy. "She told me I could have anything I liked in the shed for the bonfire. I didn't know that old thing was important. Dusty and dirty it was, and my mother so particular, I thought she'd thrown it out like the rest of the rubbish. She should have kept it in the back bedroom if it was so particular."

"It was a lovely Guy though," said Mam. "Don't worry no more - your mother would never have used it anyway - Bopa Mary Jane was built like a barn door, and you couldn't alter her dummy that much - Uncle Ben Bowen made it for her special. One thing though, that Guy Fawkes hat - I'm sure I've seen it before!"

Billy drank more cocoa, and winked at me behind his cup. Another mystery, I thought.

We had another mystery next summer, when Marged Sicncyn Oddjobs couldn't find her second best summer felt hat. Sometimes I wondered, and I know Mam did too, but there, Siencyn wouldn't have dared, would he?

CHAPTER 19

THE CHRISTMAS GOOSE

"This is going to be the best Christmas we've ever had," said Mam. "Iestyn home from foreign parts -"

"Aye, Penarth," interrupted Dadda.

"Sh!" said Mam. "And Bessie and Mog coming, and little Miss Williams, and Uncle Arthur, and Cissie Ann and Billy - how many's that?"

"What about Siencyn Oddjobs coming?" asked Dadda. "Nowhere to go he do have."

"He'll be very welcome," said Mam.

Times have changed, I thought! Used to be she couldn't abide him and his wicked ways, living in a shack on the mountain with his chickens and leaving his tidy little wife.

But all that was in the past. Since he'd helped William Lewis Amen to pray tidy at his Jubilee, Mam was all over him.

"Let's see," said Mam. "That's eleven of us altogether. I've got a tidy bit put by in the Christmas Club, so it'll be a nice big goose again this year."

I went with Dadda to Siencyn's shack to ask him to come to us for Christmas. He was so pleased he went pink, blew his nose like a high pitched trumpet.

"Well if that don't beat all. Love to come, I would. Your missus is a real good cook, and she don't stint on the gravy. But look by here, I've had a stroke of luck. My cousin up in Nelson do keep poultry, and he's giving me a goose for Christmas. What do I want with a goose? You have it - Christmas Box from me it'll be, and welcome to it."

Mam was flabbergasted when we told her. "That's real handsome," she said. "I will say this, Siencyn Oddjobs is a changed man. Adversity have refined him."

A bit later that evening she said to Dadda, "I've been thinking about the goose. If Siencyn gives us one, then all the goose money I've saved can go on something you've needed these last three years - a new overcoat."

"Will you have enough?" Dadda asked.

"Got a bit put by upstairs, I have, we'll put it on to the goose money, and go to the Fifty Shilling Tailors on Saturday."

Dadda was pleased as punch with his new overcoat. Wore it to Chapel on Sunday, he did. "I feel like a millionaire," he said. I felt so proud of him, and so did Mam too. We felt like the aristocracy of Colliery Row.

It was lovely getting ready for Christmas. I made Mam a calendar in school, and a pen wiper for Dadda, and be bought cards and presents, and Mam made lists, and worked out how much sprouts could eleven people eat, and I kept looking in the pantry at the Christmas Puddings in their basins with clean cloth covers, and the jars of pickled onions and cabbage and chutney Mam had made. The goose was arriving Christmas Eve, and so was Auntie Bessie and my new Uncle Mog - after Swansea Market shut. They were coming in Uncle Mog's van - no-one else in the street had anything faster than a bicycle - 'There's posh we are,' I thought.

We put up the trimmings and decorated the tree, and Christmas Eve I helped Mam make up the stuffing. The bread crumbs always took hours to make, rubbing the bread round and round the colander with the back of my fist. The sage smelt lovely, special and exciting. By dinner time Mam had begun to worry that the goose hadn't come.

"I hope that cousin of Siencyn's isn't going to leave it too late," said Mam.

We'd cleaned the sprouts, and made the mince pies, and the cake was on the dresser all white icing and a Father Christmas and a Robin and Holly on top.

By three o'clock Mam was really worried, and sent Dadda to find Siencyn to ask if he was sure about the goose? But Siencyn was delivering orders from Bevan's the Butchers, and Dadda couldn't find him.

At four o'clock Mam put her coat on, and stood on the door to make sure the man delivering the goose would know which house it was.

Half past four, Uncle Iestyn came and we had tea - but Mam didn't eat much.

Half past five, and Mam was in a state. "I'll never trust Siencyn Oddjobs again!" she stormed.

She scrubbed the back kitchen floor to get rid of worry that was boiling up inside her.

Six o'clock and there was a banging on the front door like an army of Bailiffs. Dadda rushed to open it.

"This twenty-five Colliery Row? Mrs Williams?"

"Yes, come you in."

"Sorry I'm late. The van had a puncture, and I have been up to my eyes."

A fat man in a dirty coat came in, smelling of cold and damp. "Here's your goose, Missus." He put the goose on the table.

We looked at the goose, and the goose looked at us.

Its bright eyes blinked, it stretched its neck and spread its wings.

"*Cato'n pawb*," said Mam. "It's alive!"

"We expected one plucked and ready to cook," said Dadda.

"Don't know nothing about that," said the man. "I was told to bring it here, and bring it here I have. Goodnight all." And he was off.

"Well," said Uncle Iestyn. "If that don't beat all."

"Now what do we do?" asked Mam.

"I'd take it off the tablecloth before it does *Ach y fi*," said Uncle Iestyn.

Dadda put his arm round the goose and picked it up. "It winked at me!" he said. "I swear it winked at me. There's a clever goose. I'll put it in the back kitchen."

"Not on my clean floor you don't," said Mam.

"I can't stand here all night holding a goose," said Dadda. "Where are you going to put it?"

"And who's going to kill it?" said Mam.

Kill it! Kill that beautiful bird that winked at Dadda! I burst into tears.

"Don't kill it," I cried. "Please don't kill it." I flung my arms around Mam and sobbed and sobbed.

"But it's our Christmas Dinner," said Mam.

"I'd rather starve," I cried.

"Don't look at me," said Dadda. "I couldn't kill it."

"Me neither," said Uncle Iestyn. "Tell you what, you put the goose in a corner of the shed - we can make a little cwtch for him with planks of wood, and I'll go down to Bailey the Bakers for some straw - he'll spare me some from his horse, I know, and I'll send Billy to Thomas Thomas' to buy some corn. You Bethan, find an old enamel basin for water and an old plate for the corn, and I'll be back in five minutes."

He picked up his cap, and rushed off. Mam said, "I think I've got something he can drink out of - What am I saying! This is our Christmas dinner I'm giving water to. If you're going out to that shed with that goose, put your coat and cap on, Megan."

I hurried to put them on, and followed Dadda down the path to the shed.

"Bring the torch, Bethan," he shouted, and Mam followed us down the garden, with a basin of water in one hand and the torch in the other. Dadda held the goose, while Mam and me made a corner safe with some old pieces of wood Dadda had been going to make something of, one day. Then gently Dadda put the goose down. It didn't seem to be very concerned with what was happening to it.

"I thought geese were supposed to be fierce?" said Mam

"This one isn't," said Dadda. "Come on, let's shut the door before it tries to fly back to Nelson."

We followed Mam and the torch back to the house. Mam sat by the table and breathed hard.

"Right," she said. "Having put the goose into Buckingham Palace, perhaps you'll tell me what we're going to have for our Christmas Dinner! Eleven people we'll be, and enough stuffing for an Ostrich, and all we've got is a tin of corned beef."

"The butcher's will still be open," said Dadda. "We can pop round and see if there's anything left."

"And what are we going to use for money?" said Mam. "You are wearing one Christmas dinner on you back, and the other one is living like a lord in the shed. We spent the goose money on your overcoat - and don't say you'll take the coat back, because the shop will be shut by now, and anyway, I've moved the buttons and sewed extra flannel lining over the shoulders. There's nothing for it, we'll have to see what's in Megan's money box!"

"I don't mind," I said. I didn't mind anything as long as they didn't kill my goose.

Dadda put a knife into the slot, and out came a pile of pennies, a half crown, sixpences, and a threepenny bit. "You can have my fag money," said Dadda, putting five pence on the table.

"If we don't go to the pictures this week, that's one and six I can put in. It don't look much, do it? I'll get my coat and hat on, and see what I can get."

"I'll come with you," said Dadda.

"No you stay here - what I'll get for this money won't weigh heavy."

She picked up her basket, and was gone... Two minutes later, here came Uncle Iestyn with a sack of straw, and cousin Billy with a bag of corn. We took the torch and went out to see my goose. It blinked at us in the light, and we put the straw down to make a warm bed, and put some corn on the enamel plate.

"That's the luckiest goose this side of Cardiff," said Billy.

"Goodnight goose," I said, and we locked the shed door and went indoors.

Dadda put the kettle on the fire, and we made some toast, and by the time Mam came back, we had a nice hot cup of tea for her and some hot supper.

"Well," she said, as she plonked her basket down on the table. "Here's our Christmas dinner." She undid the greaseproof paper and brought out a chicken.

"Bit on the small side," said Dadda.

"Small!" said Mam. "Any smaller and it'd be an egg!"

"Scrawny too!" said Uncle Iestyn.

"Eleven people have got to have a share in that, and I reckon Megan could eat it all herself," said Mam. "Look by here, what we'll do is this. Tomorrow we'll cut it up in the back kitchen, and make sure Little Miss Williams, and Uncle Arthur, and Mog and our Bessie get a fair amount, and the rest of us will make do with stuffing and the vegetables. I only hope our Cissie Ann don't say nothing!"

"You leave her to me," said Uncle Iestyn, looking fierce.

"What about supper?" said Dadda. "We can't have pickles and cold meat, that's for sure."

"I've thought of that too," said Mam. "I'll boil up the carcase, after tea, and make a good broth out of it - put carrots and onions and parsnips and a lot of potatoes - it'll be so thick we'll be able to slice it."

"We can say we thought a hot supper would be best because the weather's so cold. And you all say, 'What a good idea,' and go on that you're enjoying it. We'll have jelly and custard and tinned fruit and trifle after, so we won't starve. I can tell you this. I'll never forget *this* Christmas in a hurry. *Cato'n pawb*, look at the time. Megan not in bed, and our stockings not hung up!"

So we hung our stockings up from the rail under the mantelpiece, and Dadda wrote our names on pieces of paper and safety pinned them on.

"What about my goose hanging up his stocking?" I asked.

Mam said, "Whatever will that child say next!" but Dadda got one of my summer ankle socks and hung it up, and wrote 'Goose' on the label.

It all looked ever so exciting - I won't sleep I thought, but I slept so soundly I didn't even hear Auntie Bessie and my new Uncle Mog arriving in the van.

The next morning, I got out of bed as soon as I woke. I ran into Mam and Dadda's bedroom, but the bed was empty, and the spare room door was open, and I could see no one there, although the bed had been slept in, so I ran downstairs, and there they were in the kitchen, my Mam and Dad, and Auntie Bessie in a red jumper and my new Uncle Mog in his best suit.

"Happy Christmas!" they all called, and there was such hugging and kissing, and then Mam put a shawl over my shoulders and we opened our stockings.

Oh the bulges, and funny shapes! I had sweets and a ball and tangerine and an apple and a new penny. And Dadda and Uncle Mog had a carrot and piece of coal, and Dadda even had an old scrubbing brush that had lost its bristles.

Oh we didn't half laugh.

My goose's sock was full of corn. "I'll take it out to him now just," I said, and then opened my pillow case of presents - they were lovely, except for the libbly bodices. Aunty Scissors Ann as usual, I thought.

When the excitement had died down, I got washed and dressed in my best dark red dress with a cream lace collar that Mam had made, and we all had breakfast. Mam had made a big saucepan of porridge. "Forgot the brown sugar I have," she said. "Megan *fach*, go you into the pantry and get it."

I went into the back kitchen - oh! The warmth from the gas stove, and the smell of the dinner cooking! I went into the pantry and reached over the cold slab to get the sugar from the shelf - then I stopped and stared - there, on a plate on the slab, was the scrawny chicken. If the scrawny chicken was here, what was in the oven, cooking and sizzling away?

My stomach turned over, and a blackness came over my eyes. "My goose, they've killed it!"

I turned and went back into the kitchen, stumbling over the mat because I was so horrified I couldn't see properly.

"What's wrong with Megan?" said Mam, putting her cup of tea down quickly. "Catch her Gwyn, I think she's going to faint!"

Dadda took me on his lap, and held my head down, and Mam rushed to the cupboard where we kept the brandy and they gave me some. "What's the matter, *cariad?*" said Auntie Bessie.

"My goose," I said. "You killed it. You promised you wouldn't," and I hid my face in my hands.

"No we didn't," said Dadda. "Your goose is right as rain. Feed him after breakfast we will."

"What's in the oven then?" I asked. "It's not the scrawny chicken!"

"Well fancy her noticing that!" said Auntie Bessie. "Too sharp by half she is."

"It's a surprise," said Mam. "A lovely surprise. You tell her Mog."

So my new Uncle Mog said, "We was keeping this surprise till later - but I'll tell you now. See, when it was time to shut the stall last night, one of the butchers in the market came to me and said he'd got some poultry left over - ordered for, it was, but the man hadn't come for it, so would I swop him a big piece of ham for the bird - so I did, and that's what's in the oven! And you'll never guess what it is - it's a Turkey!"

A turkey! I'd never ever seen a turkey.

"Yes," said Mam. "We was all up at five o'clock this morning to stuff it, and start cooking it - it takes hours it do, and none of us have ever cooked a turkey before, but that's what's in the oven! We wouldn't kill your goose, *cariad*."

"'Course not," said Dadda.

"You'd better take her and see," said my new Uncle Mog. "She won't be better till she've seen her goose."

"Breakfast first," said Mam.

"She won't eat her breakfast till she's got her mind at rest," said Dadda, so we got my wellingtons, and my cap and coat and we all went down to the bottom of the garden to the shed. Dadda unlocked the door.

"Here he is, safe and sound," he said. "Come on, move over, let Megan see you. Hey! What's this? Your goose isn't a him - it's a her - look! She've laid you a Christmas present, and he held up an egg with a pink ribbon on it.

I was so happy and excited, I began to cry.

"All this excitement," said Mam, marching me back into the house. "Now eat all our porridge, before you catch a chill on an empty stomach."

Oh! What a Christmas Day that was. Went by in a flash it did. Carols in Chapel, and me with my new handbag and hankie with Devon Violets scent on it, then home where half the women in the street had come to see the turkey and admire the size, and Dadda taking the scrawny chicken to Mrs Jones Ty Top, because Mr Jones was on the dole. Then Little Miss Williams coming with a bottle of Ginger Wine and a nice box of liquorice all sorts, and Uncle Arthur dumped by his sister, who looked forward all year to us having him for one day, and Oddjobs arriving in his best russet Harris Tweed suit with a nose to match.

"Happy Christmas Siencyn," said Dadda. "Come you in and look at the

146

goose you gave us." And there, looking through the kitchen window, we saw Uncle Iestyn and Billy exercising the goose in the back garden.

"Well," said Siencyn. "I never knew it was going to be a *live* goose, when I said you could have it."

"And it laid an egg for me too," I said, showing the egg in cotton wool in a dish on the dresser.

"Lays eggs too," said Siencyn. "That's not what I had in mind when I gave it to you. Didn't know he'd send his best layer."

Clear as crystal, I knew Siencyn wanted the goose back. I tugged at his jacket, he bent down, and quick as a flash I had my arms round his neck and kissed him on his cheek. It was like sandpaper, and he smelled of wood smoke and the smell you get when you pass a Pub.

"Oh thank you for my goose," I cried. "Best present I ever had. Oh! You are kind!"

"Yes indeed," said Mam. "Very generous." And she shook hands with him, and so did Dadda and my new Uncle Mog and they said how kind and warm-hearted he was and I thought, 'Good, he'll never have the nerve to ask for the goose back now!' He looked pleased and pink, and he swayed with emotion.

You should have seen the dinner table! All squashed round on chairs from every room in the house, and the turkey so big Dadda and my new Uncle Mog had to carry it in between them, and Mam kept telling everybody she'd never cooked a turkey before and was it all right? and everybody's plate piled with stuffing and potatoes and sprouts and swede and heaps of turkey.

"Lovely, really lovely."

"Enjoying this a treat, I am."

"More gravy? More stuffing, more turkey?"

Then the pudding and I found the silver threepence, and cups and cups of tea, and all the ladies clearing away the dishes and the men in the parlour smoking cigars as if they was used to doing it every day of their lives.

Oh! The lovely rich smell. Bye and bye the talking got quieter, and the snores got louder, till Mam called us all to have a cup of tea and a mince pie and Christmas cake and Mam gave me the Father Christmas off the top.

After we'd fed my goose and shut her up for the night all warm and comfy. We got round the piano, and sang. Everybody did something. Little Miss Williams sang that her 'Love was like a red red rose' - she did that every year - and Uncle Iestyn sang that 'A Sailor's Life was Jolly' so Aunty Scissors Ann sent cousin Billy home to get a bottle of Elderberry wine, probably in case he felt he'd like to wander off again, I thought. Cousin Billy said he couldn't remember if his mother said Elderberry or Blackberry wine, so he brought both!

We all had a taste of each of them. "It's not as if it was alcohol, said Aunty Scissors Ann. "Homemade, this is." And the singing went very well after that - Asleep in the Deep and the Bold Gendarmes and the Three Little Maids from School. My new uncle Mog got a bit sad when he sang a song he remembered his grandfather singing, so we had more Welsh Hymns to cheer us up - Diadem and *I bob un sy'n ffyddlon*, and Calon Lan.

Then, "Supper," said Mam, and there it was laid in the kitchen, slices of cold turkey thick as you like, and pickled onions big as my fist, and pickled cabbage and two kinds of chutney, and bread and butter spread thick. Then trifle, and jelly and custard and tinned fruit and more mince pies and cake and gallons of tea.

We ate and talked and joked, even Uncle Arthur smiled, and Siencyn got redder and redder in the face and he couldn't stop grinning. At last we could eat no more, and we sat drinking a last cup of tea.

"Best Christmas I ever had Missus," said Siencyn. "You're a tidy little cook."

Mam blushed and smiled and nodded. "Hear, hear," everybody said - even Aunty Scissors Ann had softened.

"Well," said Dadda. "I tell you this. I don't think nobody, not even the King hisself in Buckingham Palace have had a better Christmas than we've had, and I tell you something else, there's no family in the whole of Wales had a Turkey *and* a Goose for Christmas."

CHAPTER 20

SUCH HEAVY SNOW

I could never remember before that, we had so much snow. It snowed for one whole night and one whole day, and it was so cold that the water in my cup by the bed, had ice on the top of it when I woke up in the morning.

Dad had to clear a path out the back for us to go to the lav, and a bit by the front door for people to walk on.

The sky was blue as summer and the snow was so white it made your eyes ache.

Dad put his wellingtons on, and his big coat and muffler. "I'm going up to see Siencyn Oddjobs," he told Mam. "Worried I am about him."

Mam said, "You'd better take some bread and milk up with you. And you be careful. Don't stop there long or I'll be worried."

"I hope he's all right," said Dadda as he went off down the road. Mam looked worried all the morning.

The Baker couldn't come with the bread, because he snow was too deep for the horse and cart, so we had to go round to Bailey the Bakers ourselves. The milk wouldn't come neither, so we had to go round to Mrs Willams with our jugs.

"No milk!" said Mrs Williams. "The farmer must be snowed up there on the hills." It was all very exciting and best of all - there was no school and we had to have condensed milk.

It was nearly dark by the time Dad came home. Mam pounced on him like a cat on a mouse.

"Where've you been, worrying me out of my mind," she said as she unwrapped him from his overcoat. "Look at the state of you, trousers sopping wet, and looking frozen to the marrow, and tired out."

In no time he was pulled and pushed into dry clothes, his feet in a bowl of mustard and hot water, and a dish of boiled onions on a tray as he sat by the fire.

"Now tell me all about it," said Mam.

"It's not good," said Dadda. "Lucky I met Iestyn, and he came with me. Awful job we had, getting to the shack, took us hours. When we got there, there was Siencyn lying on the floor, breathing bad, and no fire going. He'd had a fall when he was going to get more coal, and hurt his leg. I think he must have knocked hisself out, and the cold was so bad, and the window broke, and snow coming in. We wrapped him in a blanket and carried him down to the nearest house, and the upshot was, he's in hospital with a broken ankle and bronchitis which could turn to pneumonia."

"He's not going to die, is he?" I asked.

"No, no *cariad*," said Mam.

But I knew she wasn't telling the truth. I don't think we slept much that night, and early next morning, Dadda went off to see how Siencyn was.

It was touch and go for a bit, and I couldn't enjoy the snow no more. Mam and Dad went to the shack to get clean nightshirts for him to look tidy in hospital, and found a terrible mess.

The snow had brought the roof down, and most of the furniture was smashed and all his clothes was scattered around and wet. Mam brought his russet suit and his best overcoat, and sponged and pressed them, and put them to air, but she said his nightshirts and drawers were a disgrace. She sent Dadda up to the hospital with my grampa's flannel things that had been kept proper in mothballs in the chest in drawers in the back bedroom.

After the snow came the thaw, and it rained, and we had awful storms.

One day, Dadda came in and said, "Well that's the end of that old shack. The weather have really ruined it."

"Oh, there's sad," I said. I loved that old shack, with the fox in the glass case, and the red velvet valance, with bobbles that was scorched and smoky over the mantelpiece, and the two pictures: 'Bear ye one another's Burdens,' and 'Where your treasure is, There will your heart be also,' and the text with roses, 'Thou God See-est Me'.

"Good riddance to bad rubbish," snapped Aunty Scissors Ann. "The Council should have ought to condemn it years ago."

A SHED, CHICKENS, SIENCYN AND ME

"It was a lovely shack," I said.

"Nonsense," said Aunty Scissors Ann, warming her feet on the fender. "Dirty old place it was. *Ach y fi.*"

"It was a man's home," said Mam, all quiet.

"Well anyway, he's getting better, isn't he? Saved his life Gwyn and Iestyn did, but they won't get no thanks for it."

"He's looking old and tired," said Dadda.

"Humph," said Aunty Scissors Ann.

Mam got out her mixing bowl and the flour.

"What you making?" asked Aunty Scissors Ann.

"I thought I'd just do a few fancy cakes for Gwyn to take up to the hospital," said Mam, greasing the tins.

"If that don't beat all," said Aunty Scissors Ann. "Catch me making cakes for that old scallywag."

"Catch you doing nothing for nobody," said Dadda very quiet.

"I heard that," said Aunty Scissors Ann.

Siencyn was getting better slowly, and at last Dadda and Mam took me to see him. I couldn't go into the hospital because I was too young, but Dadda lifted me up so I could look through the window of the ward. There was a lot of beds there, and people visiting, and nurses with starched aprons and caps. Mam was standing by the bed of a frail old man. She waved at me, said something to the old man, and he looked up, all slow like, and waved as well.

"Who's that?" I asked Dadda.

"That's Siencyn," he said.

When Mam came out to us, Dadda was still wiping my eyes and saying, "It's all right, don't cry," and, "If you don't stop crying, you'll have me at it too."

We called in Aunty Scissors Ann and Uncle Iestyn'n on the way home.

"How is he?" asked Uncle Iestyn.

"Much better, and he'll be allowed home soon, but what'll happen then, the Dear Above knows," said Dadda.

"Anybody told him that his shack's gone?" asked Uncle Iestyn.

"I haven't had the heart to, but I think he guesses. He seems to have lost interest in going on living."

"Where's he going to go then?" asked Aunty Scissors Ann.

"Work house, I suppose. I can't see Marged taking him back now. Need a lot of looking after, he will, that is, if he lasts that long. Workhouse is the only place for him."

151

"Don't talk like that," said Dadda. "We'll have to look for nice lodgings for him."

"Well don't look at me," said Aunty Scissors Ann. "Pity you didn't come before, I made a nice cup of tea, but it's gone cold now."

"Don't bother," snapped Mam. "We got plenty of tea in our house." And she got Dad and me out of there and into our own house before you could say 'Jack Robinson'.

Dadda and Uncle Iestyn went all round the houses, looking for lodgings for Siencyn, but no luck.

"Can understand it, can't you?" said Uncle Iestyn. "All these houses is small, and nearly everybody's got kids or a Grannie or Granpa living with them. Thought we'd be lucky with Miss Evans Preswylfa. Two spare bedrooms she do have, but she said she couldn't have a man lodger, or people would talk."

"But she's gone eighty!" said Mam.

"I know," grinned Dadda. "But she said she've lived without a man all them years, and she didn't want to risk being called a Jezebel at her age!"

"Now, what do we do?" asked Uncle Iestyn.

"Keep trying," said Mam.

But when the day came and Siencyn was due to leave the hospital, there was still nowhere.

That day, my new Uncle Mog and Auntie Bessie were going to get eggs from Brecon, so they said they would come over from Swansea in the morning, and then bring Siencyn to our house in their van, and stay with us for the night and get the eggs next day. When I got home from school they were there. I knew they'd come, because the van was outside our door. It had 'Mog Jones. Butter Merchant. New Laid Eggs A Speciality' in letters this big on the side.

They were all in the kitchen when I got in, Mam and Dad, Uncle Iestyn cousin Billy, Aunty Bessie and my new Uncle Mog. And in the armchair by the fire, a little grey old man in a Harris Tweed suit that looked as if it belonged to somebody bigger.

Aunty Bessie and my new Uncle Mog gave me such big hugs and kisses, I nearly couldn't breathe.

"Aren't you going to give Siencyn a kiss?" asked Dadda. Siencyn's that poor little old man with the dull eyes - that was Siencyn! Siencyn, on his way to the Workhouse, with a brown paper parcel with my Grampa's nightshirts in it. Suddenly, I felt frightened.

"If somebody looked in my waistcoat pocket, I think they'd find Chocolate Drops," said my new Uncle Mog, but even chocolate drops couldn't help.

There was a click on the back door latch, and Aunty Scissors Ann came in, all gimlet eyes and beaky nose.

"Oh, so you are all here I see. Thought I heard the van." She saw Siencyn. "You've led everybody a merry dance, by all accounts. Getting people worried, and putting people out. You won't be allowed to behave like that where you are going." She smiled at him, like a thin knife stabbing in the back.

"And where is he going?" asked Mam.

"Why, to the Workhouse, of course. He'll be looked after there."

"There'll be no Workhouse for nobody while I live and breathe," said Mam, putting her hand on Siencyn's shoulder.

"Don't tell me he have found lodgings," said Aunty Scissors Ann sounding disappointed.

"No, he haven't found lodgings," said Mam.

"Marged never wants him back after the way he have treated her." Aunty Scissors Ann was shocked.

"Siencyn doesn't want to live with her, after the way she have treated him. If a man leaves home, it's usually because his wife has made his home a misery to him."

I heard Dad say under his breath, "Good for you, Bethan."

"I don't know nothing about that," said Aunty Scissors Ann, red as a turkey cock, her eyes sharp as you please. "If he've not found lodgings, or if he's not going back to his poor, tidy little wife, and he's too high and mighty for the Workhouse, where is he going, may I ask?"

"He's not going nowhere," said Mam. "He's staying here, with us. He haven't found lodgings because he've found a home, and a family, where he's wanted. He's going to have the back bedroom."

Aunty Scissors Ann sat down as if she'd been hit on the head with a mallet.

"You are having that - that - that rapscallion to live here, with you! You want your head read. Don't expect me to come running round here helping out when he gets too much for you. Just wait till Marged hears about this. She'll laugh herself silly."

"Marged Jenkins is a mean, spiteful, back biting old witch." I could see Mam was getting her moss off now. "The way she's treating her poor sister is the talk of Abercynon - and after her sister has been good enough to give her a home. There's only one woman on God's earth worse than Siencyn's wife, and that's you, Cissie Ann Williams. And I tell you one thing more, keep on the way you're going, and *your* husband will be off again, but this time, there's none of us going to keep your secret and say Iestyn's been drowned at sea - we'll tell the world he've left home because you are a misery to live with, and I'll make sure everybody from Taff's Well to Tonypandy knows the kind of woman you are."

"And if my father leaves home, this time I go with him," said Billy, looking fierce.

Aunty Scissors Ann stood up, breathing like a dragon. "Thank you. Thank you for insulting me like that. But don't start moaning to me that your Bessie and your Mog have got nowhere to sleep tonight, because Siencyn Oddjobs is in your spare bedroom. See how you manage then!"

"They're having Megan's bedroom, and Megan's sleeping down on the couch tonight."

"Oooh! lovely," I said.

"No need for that," said Uncle Iestyn, looking brave as a lion. "They can sleep in our back bedroom."

"The bed's not aired." Aunty Scissors Ann was spitting mad now.

"Then air it," said Uncle Iestyn.

"We'll see Bessie and Mog later then." Here was Uncle Iestyn, the size of a pygmy, growing into a giant. "Come on, Cissie Ann. We'll go home and have our tea. I just fancy a nice sardine sandwich, and a piece of cake."

"There isn't any cake." Aunty Scissors Ann was down, but not out.

"Then make some, woman."

I'd never heard Uncle Iestyn call her a 'woman' before.

"I fancy a Teisen Lap, and don't be stingy with the sultanas. Come on."

And off went Aunty Scissors Ann, meek as a lamb, with Billy grinning all over his face.

As he shut the back door, Uncle Iestyn winked at us.

"Ooph!" said Dadda. "I never lived through ten minutes like that in all my life."

"I don't often kiss women," said my new Uncle Mog. "But I'm going to kiss you now, Bethan Williams. Well done." And he gave Mam a big smacking kiss on her cheek.

"Oh go on with you," she said, pushing him away, all pink and pleased, and pretending she was neither.

"I've wanted to say that for years, and I feel better now. Come on Siencyn, I'll take you up to your bedroom, and then we can all have tea."

"Now wait a minute," said Auntie Bessie. "Mog and me will put tea - some lovely ham we've brought, so we'll fry that, and have ham and eggs for tea."

Siencyn turned his head and looked at her. "And fried bread?" he asked.

"And fried bread," said Auntie Bessie. "And we've brought a big piece of Dundee cake, and some of the pink and yellow slab cake that Megan likes."

"With real pretending cream, is it?" I asked.

"Yes, real thick pretending cream," said Auntie Bessie. "Come on, Mog, let's get started. I'm starving."

"She always is," said my new Uncle Mog, looking at her so proud.

"I'll put more coal on the fire," said Dadda. "Get it all warm and lovely." He and Mam looked at each other, and smiled as if they shared a lovely secret. I always felt happy when I saw that look.

"Come on then, Siencyn," said Mam. "Megan carry his parcel up for me, will you? Careful now, don't go up the stairs too quick."

I followed them upstairs to the back bedroom. Mam opened the door wide, and we went in. I gasped! There on the bed was the patchwork quilt from Siencyn's shack, all clean and ironed beautiful, and the colours that bright and pretty. On the chest in drawers was the fox in a new glass case Dad had made, the glass shining so clear you'd think the fox was winking at you, and above it, the two pictures, 'Bear ye one another's Burdens,' and 'Where your Treasure is, There will your Heart be also,' the black smoke gone from the glass, and the wood glowing like conkers the first time you take them out of their prickly cases. Even the text was there, above the bed - 'Thou God see-est me' - and the roses round the words red and yellow like it was a summer's day. On the table by the bed was Lizzie May's Owl. Mam had even give him the rag rug she'd just finished, all new and fresh, by the bed, so he wouldn't get his feet cold on the oil cloth when he got out of bed.

Siencyn was open mouthed. The nasty grey colour was going from his face, and his eyes didn't look so empty.

"This is like a Palace, Missus," he said. "And you got my best things too! I don't know what to say."

"Now then," said Mam, all brisk. "I've put your shirts in the top draw, and keep your socks by here - you're a bit short of them at the moment, but I've got some more on my needles for you. And hang your overcoat and suit up tidy in the wardrobe, and I don't want no toffee papers on the floor. And don't think you're going to live the life of Riley by here. I could do with the outside pantry having a nice coat of whitewash, and I want you to paper Megan's bedroom for her. I've seen nice paper in Ponty with Micky Mouse on it. It'll do lovely."

"Micky Mouse." Siencyn looked tickled pink. "I've never papered with Micky Mouse paper before, but I'll do you a good job."

"Well, when you're feeling stronger, we'll go to Ponty on the bus and get some. And look by here." Mam pointed out of the window. "I know it's getting dark but you can just see the shed where Megan's goose do live. Well, I was thinking, what about building another bit on to it, and having a run with wire netting, we could keep chickens, save us buying eggs."

"Chickens!" Siencyn's face lit up like a Christmas tree. "Aye, we could," he said. "I could go down the *Co-op* yard - I know the foreman - he'll let me have the wood cheap, and a nice little bit of corrugated iron for the roof. Wouldn't cost much it wouldn't."

"Where'll we get the chickens?" asked Mam, looking serious, but with her eyes all twinkling and dancing.

"Maggie the Lan - that's where we'll go. How many do you think?" said Siencyn.

"Start with six hens at point of lay," said Mam. "And see how we go." "Now you get better quick, and we'll have them chickens as soon as you're able to see to them."

Siencyn was all smiles. It was like looking at a miracle, like a bud opening out and blossoming into a flower. He seemed to grow bigger and younger by the minute.

"Come on then," said Mam. "Time for tea." And we went down stairs, Siencyn murmuring happily to himself, "Six hens at point of lay - aye, that's the thing, and see how we go."

In the kitchen, Dadda had made up the fire, and lit the gaslight and the table was laid and the kettle singing on the hob. Here comes Auntie Bessie and Uncle Mog from the back kitchen, with plates of lovely ham and eggs and fried bread.

"Sit down, sit down," said Mam, so we all did. There was fresh white crusty bread on the table to mop up the fat, and a jar of chutney, and a bottle of tomato sauce. What a feast!

"Now," said Mam. "Megan, will you say Grace?" so I did.

"Thank you for the world so sweet,
Thank you for the food we eat,
Thank you for the birds that sing,
Thank you God for everything."

Siencyn said, "Amen." And the he added, "My cup runneth over," and he dipped his fried bread in the runny egg and ate it.

And so he lived with us, and Mam bullied him, and made him take cod liver oil and malt every morning, and wouldn't let him leave off his flannel shirts till May was out. And we had six chickens, and I had Mickey Mouse wallpaper in my bedroom, and Siencyn came to Chapel on Sundays in his clean, pressed russet suit and shining collar, and went to sleep in the sermon.

Once or twice Aunty Scissors Ann told Mam that Siencyn had been back-sliding in the Red Cow. "He's reeking of Extra Strong Mints," she said, but Mam said, "Nonsense, I gave him the mints because he had dyspepsia," and later on I heard her tell Dadda that she'd rather Siencyn drunk than Aunty Scissors Ann sober, and Uncle Iestyn heard it and said, "Me too!"

Then cousin Billy started courting a nice girl from Porth, she had been to the County School and Aunty Scissors Ann was so proud that Billy was going up in the world, that she had her hair permed and bought half a dozen pastry forks, and mellowed beautiful.

And so, except for a few hiccups now and then - like they say in the books - we all lived happily ever after - nearly.

APPENDIX

There are two more stories I want to include in this book, the first is another Siencyn story; as it's another story about Christmas it does not chronologically fit into the main text.

The second is a memory my mother had as a young girl, a true story which I hope it puts all the Siencyn stories into context. The story I believe is a real and it's what happened in her village one afternoon and how it affected her and shows it the poverty and desperation there was at this time. It's hard to imagine anything like this happening in today society and I thank God for that.

THE MATCHMAKER

Once Guy Fawkes Night was over Mam really got in her stride for Christmas. She made lists – who was to get a present, who was to get a card, and who was to be visited and given mince pies or bags or boiled sweets?

Not toffees, not with their teeth. No, boiled sweets it was to be. They could share them with Idwal and Auntie Gwyneth, and sucking pear drops didn't depend on whether you had teeth or not.

She worried over the Christmas cake till it came out of the oven cooked beautiful and smelling like a dozen Eastern Spice Shops. The day the puddings were boiled we could hardly see each other for steam. Then Mam worried about the sprouts.

There were the usual people coming – Auntie Bessie and my new Uncle Mog, Auntie Scissors Anne and Uncle Iestyn and Billy and his young lady. She was a lovely girl and had been to County School. Auntie Scissors Anne thought she really added class to the family, and bought packets of doyleys and a tray cloth with poppies on it. Whether it was the young lady or the doyleys. Auntie Scissors Anne had really mellowed. Then there was Uncle Arthur and little Miss Williams, because they always came, and me and Mam and Dadda, and Siencyn because he lived with us now that he didn't have his shack because of the snow last January.

"That's twelve," said Mam. "Now how much sprouts do twelve people eat?"

She weighed ten sprouts on her weighing scales, multiplied b twelve, added two pounds to make sure, and got the sum wrong and had to do it again.

Roast Parsnips to go with the pork that Auntie Bessie and my new Uncle Mog would bring from Swansea Market after they had shut their butter and cheese stall for the holidays, didn't worry Mam at all – it was only sprouts that got her all flummoxed. She made chutney – jars of it and pickled onions and red cabbage and her own mincemeat.

We had secret parcels hidden in the drawers and the tops of wardrobes and Siencyn was more excited about Christmas than any of us.

"*Darro di*," he said. "I haven't hanged up my stocking for Father Christmas this year." And he too started to hide knobbly parcels in his bedroom. He took his Cod Liver Oil every morning without a murmur, and ran errands for Mam looking important.

One Saturday morning in December, Mam gave Siencyn a list of things she wanted from the shops – vegetables for the weekend, new rubber heels for my school shoes, Robin Starch and a bar of carbolic soap. She also gave him strict instructions that as the weather was parky, he was to go to Bracchi's for a drink of hot Oxo before he picked up the swede and the savoy. He was to keep his muffler tidy round his neck and be sure to have a clean hankie, and she sent him off with a fish frail to carry things in, a purse with money, and warned him about any traffic that might be about.

Dinner was nearly ready by the time he came home with the shopping. His nose was red as a beetroot, and he was glad to warm himself by the fire as Mam unpacked the fish frail.

"You remembered your hot Oxo then?" she asked. "See anybody you knew in Bracchi's?"

"Yes I did," said Siencyn, putting on his slippers that Mam had been warming for him on the fender. "Oh yes I did, and I tell you now, I'm really worried. I had my hot Oxo at the same table as Uncle Arthur, and he was eating dinner there!"

"Eating dinner," said Mam. "What call did he have to have his dinner there?"

"I know," said Siencyn. "And not only that, but his cuffs was frayed and so was his collar."

"Never!" said Mam. "Where's his sister then? She must be bad in bed to neglect him like that."

"That's the point," said Siencyn. "She's not looking after him no more because she's not there! She've gone off to be a missionary."

Mam sat down with a 'plop'.

"A missionary, where've she gone to then?"

"Swansea," said Siencyn.

"Swansea!" said Mam. "I'd have thought there was enough chapels in Swansea without her going there."

"I think it's something to do with that lot up by Pretoria Street," said Siencyn. "The League of Total Teetotallers – that's what Uncle Arthur said."

"We'll have to think about this," said Mam.

Dadda was working nights, so we waited until he came down stairs from his sleep and then we all had Mam's thick broth with crusty bread to dip in it. It was a lovely dinner, and after that I took my crayoning book and my crayons to the windowsill while I knelt up on the sofa to colour in a robin redbreast.

After the dishes was all washed up tidy in the back kitchen, Mam plonked herself down by the table and made Dadda and Siencyn come and sit there too. She'd put the chenille cloth on the table, and had a pencil and notebook. No one took any notice of me.

"Now then," said Mam. "Siencyn, is Uncle Arthur's sister ever going to come back again? Perhaps this is only for now, like?"

"Not according to Uncle Arthur," said Siencyn. "She have left him for good, and is going to reform the whole South Wales before going on to America to make everybody there a Total Teetotaller too!"

Dadda chuckled. "I bet the Welsh Brewers are shaking in their shoes," he said.

"That does it," said Mam. "We have got to help Uncle Arthur, and the best way – in fact – in fact the only way, is to get him a wife!"

"What if he don't want a wife?" asked Siencyn.

"If Mam says he wants a wife, he wants a wife," said Dadda.

"Now," said Mam. "Let's draw up a list of candidates. Nobody under forty or over sixty. She must be clean and tidy and respectable, and a good cook. A widow without children would do or an unmarried lady. And she should really ought to be Chapel."

"Blonde or brunette?" asked Dadda.

"Don't matter," said Mam. "As long as she have got some hair, she'll do." There was a silence, then Mam said, "What about Mary Davies the Bwlch?"

"Too mean," said Siencyn.

"Phyllis Francis?"

"Too miserable," said Dadda.

"Annie Thomas Top House?"

"No," said Siencyn. "Don't stop talking she don't. You'd have to give her gob stoppers to shut her up."

"Lizzie Little?"

"She's so fussy in the house she'd be dusting Uncle Arthur like she do dust them china vases in her front room. Dusted the patterns off them she have."

"Beatty Davies?"

"*No*," said Dadda and Siencyn together.

"Why?" asked Mam. "What's wrong with Beatty Davies?"

"Never you mind," said Dadda. "Who's next?"

"Well what about Catrin Edwards?" asked Mam, sounding desperate.

There was a pause and then Dadda said, "She might do."

Mam went on. "She have looked after her father all them years, and then her three brothers. The last one's only just left home to get married. She do know how to cook and clean and keep a man tidy."

"You want more than that," said Dadda. "I didn't marry you because you could cook and clean and keep me tidy!"

"That was different," said Mam. "Look, all I'll do is to ask Catrin Edwards to come to us for Christmas Day, and see if she do take to Uncle Arthur."

"And if *he* do take to her," said Dadda. "Look – he have been a bachelor all them years, perhaps he do like it that way."

"We'll see," said Mam. "And remember mum's the word."

"Mum's the word," said Dadda.

"Me too," said Siencyn.

The first hiccup in Mam's plan came when Catrin Edwards said she already promised to go somewhere for Christmas dinner, but she wouldn't mind coming to us after tea. "See you about six," she told Mam when we met her on the way to the pictures on Friday.

On our way home, Dadda said he thought she was too big and bouncy for Uncle Arthur. But Mam said marriage could alter that. "We'll just have to do our best for Uncle Arthur on Christmas Day between tea time and supper. If only it could be love at first sight."

"First sight," said Dadda. "They was in the same class in the Infant's School!"

Mam was beginning to look down in the mouth

I saw Uncle Arthur in chapel on Sunday – he looked just the same as always, quiet and grey and squashed. There was too much to think of to wonder if Mam's plan was any good. I just got on with re-arranging my box of presents for everybody – pen wipers and kettle holders, and a bar of chocolate for Cousin Billy and one for his young lady, and a bottle of

Californian Poppy scent for Mam and in the fancy stall at the chapel sisterhood I bought a pin cushion for Siencyn with 'Welcome little stranger' on it, all spelt out in pins. For Dadda I bought a packet of woodbines. It was so exciting.

By Christmas Eve our house looked like a palace with paper chains on the ceilings and pretty cards on the mantelpiece, and nuts and tangerines, and box of dates. In the pantry on the cold stone slab was all the vegetables, and the big tin for the joint all ready with a bowl of dripping next to it. Even more exciting, I was going to sleep with Mam while Dadda slept on the sofa downstairs and Auntie Bessie and my new Uncle Mog had my bedroom.

As it began to get dark, Mam hopefully put mistletoe up in the middle room and just inside the front door. "There," she said to Dadda. "Let's see if that'll help matters along. Now where did I put them crackers?"

'Why does she want them crackers tonight?' I thought.

I went on writing out names to pin on our stockings to hand up over the fire place, but out of the corner of my eye, I saw Mam slip something inside one of the crackers, and she made a little mark on the outside so she'd know which one it was.

'It's a surprise for me,' I thought – just like I always get the silver threepence out of the Christmas pudding.

I couldn't wait to go to bed so that Christmas would come quicker. It was lovely getting into Mam's bed, all warm from the hot brick wrapped in flannel and lumpy as bread dough put near the warmth to rise. I slept so soundly I didn't hear Auntie Bessie and my new Uncle Mog's van arrive. As soon as I awoke, I hurried to the window. There it was outside our home, 'MOG JONES BUTTER MERCHANT NEW LAID EGGS A SPECIALITY' on the side, parked right by our front door for all the neighbours to admire.

I ran downstairs, and there was hugging and kissing from all the family, and Siencyn too – he hadn't shaved yet and was very whiskery. He was pink with pleasure.

"Stockings and presents first," said Mam, so we looked into our own stockings and found nuts and tangerines, and I had a new shinning ha'penny in the toe.

Then the presents – I had all I'd ever dreamed of, and not a liberty bodice in Sight. There was books too. One was called *Little Women* – 'I expect that's about dwarfs,' I thought. Even my goose's socks was full – full of golden corn.

Then the breakfast, with Auntie Bessie and my new Uncle Mog carrying plates of bacon and egg and fried bread from the back kitchen. There was so much excitement that Mam packed Dadda and Siencyn and my new

Uncle Mog and me off to Chapel to quieten us down.

On the way home we met Uncle Arthur on his way to our house. He looked very tidy and perhaps he didn't need a wife after all, I thought. When he got home and he took his overcoat off, I could see he was wearing his best suit and tie, and a shirt without no frayed edges, and he'd polished his shoes and he gave us a big piece of shop bought slab cake, yellow and pink with real pretending cream in it. The Auntie Scissors Anne came – her new perm was so tight it looked like her hair was all knobs and screwed to her head, Uncle Iestyn and cousin Billy and his young lady Ceridwen O'Connor – her Grampa had been Irish, but she was Welsh like us – and last of all, little Miss Williams with a bottle of Ginger Wine and a box of Liquorice All Sorts.

"No harm in Ginger Wine," said Mam.

We got down to our Christmas dinner very quick – "No need hanging about," said Mam, so we sat down and admired the tablecloth and the crackers – I was surprised they was not the ones I'd seen Mam fiddling with – and we pulled the crackers and put on the hats and read the riddles and jokes and then Mam and Auntie Bessie brought in the food.

It was smelling wonderful, ad our plates was piled up with the roast pork and the stuffing and the roast potatoes and parsnips and fluffy mashed potatoes and the sprouts – Mam had gone overboard this year – we had enough sprouts to last till February, and there was thick, hot gravy. We said Grace, then silence fell as we tucked in. When we got our breath back there was the pudding and hot custard – I had the silver threepence – and after cups of tea the women washed up and tidied everything, and the men dozed by the fire, and the winter's afternoon became darker outside. I read my new book – Little Women wasn't about dwarfs, and cousin Billy and Ceridwen went off to spend the rest of the day with Ceridwen's family. Mam kept glancing at the clock. "Bit early for Catrin Edwards," she said, so we all had a cup in hand, and a mince pie and everybody got their second wind.

It began to rain at half past five and Mam looked worried. What if it was too wet for Catrin Edwards to come? What if the Plan couldn't get off the ground?

Uncle Arthur looked happy enough, sitting by Uncle Iestyn and talking Rugby – they was arranging the Welsh team for when the Internationals started.

Catrin Edwards came at six o'clock – refused any tea or mince pies. "I'd bust," she said, so Mam said we all had to go into the front room to sing. Auntie Scissors Anne and Uncle Iestyn came round with glasses of elderberry wine to get us going.

"It's not as if it's alcohol," said Auntie Scissors Anne. "It's homemade, it is!"

Mam sat at the piano, and off we went. Uncle Iestyn and Dadda sang 'The Bold Gendarmes', wearing funny policeman's hats on their heads; Auntie Bessie and my new Uncle Mog sang 'Trot Here and There'; Scissors Anne and Mam sang 'Three Little Maids from School', then we all sang Calon Lan to give everybody a go – but Oh dear! We found that Catrin Edwards had a voice like a foghorn! It was low and booming and terrible. Mam looked worried.

Then I sang 'Oh the Good Ship *Lollipop*', then it was little Miss Williams turn. She always sang 'My love is like a red red rose', but this time she brought music for a different song. It was called 'Let the great big world keep turning, never mind if I have you'. It sounded really nice. Then we all sang carols and had more wine, but Catrin Edwards drowned not only the sopranos but the tenors and basses as well! Then supper – cold roast pork and chutney and pickles all set out like a feast. Mam told everybody where to sit and she put Catrin Edwards next to Uncle Arthur. We pulled our crackers – and I saw what was in Uncle Arthur's cracker – a diamond ring out of *Woolworths'* sixpenny tray! 'That's for me,' I thought, but although Uncle Arthur put on his paper hat and read out his joke, he didn't give me the ring! There's disappointed I was!

As we all ate, Mam began the opening of her great campaign.

"Catrin, there's lonely you must be now your brothers have all gone, living all alone like that."

Catrin Edwards crushed a pickled onion, swallowed it and dribbled a bit of vinegar. "No blooming fear," she said. "Glad I am to see the back of the lot of them."

Mam looked taken aback. "What about the jobs about the house, carrying coal and whitening the pantry and chopping sticks?" she asked.

"I don't miss none of that, because I always done them things myself. The lazy lot never did nothing in the house. I've cooked and cleaned and done their shoes and darned and mended and white washed and painted too. There's not a job about the house I can't do, so I don't miss none of them. I tried hard to get that lot married off and now I live the life of Riley. And I don't miss no money neither – got a nice little job with Mr Evan John Jones Paris House – don't get my hands dirty, and I get all the gossip. MEN! NO THANK YOU. I'm have a real good time without them – pass me more of them pickles, Megan. There's a good girl."

I handed the dish of pickled onions to her and she took a big lot of them. "I do love pickled onions," she said, and scrunched another big one.

Mam looked all squashed, as if she'd been sat on.

"Eat up everybody," said Dadda, so we did and Catrin Edwards ate and laughed and had more elderberry wine and two helpings of trifle and a big slice of Christmas cake. We talked and laughed and my New Uncle Mog told us funny stories about the people he met in Swansea Market. He never mentions Uncle Arthur's sister and the League of Total Teetotallers. Perhaps they'd already gone further west, I thought. Mam sat all quiet. Her Plan was gone down the drain.

At last Catrin Edwards said. "Look at the time! Ten o'clock, and I promised to look in on the Miss Pughses. Now where's my mac and umbrella?"

"In the passage," said Mam. "I'll see you out."

When Catrin Edwards had got her mac and hat on, she poked her head round the middle room door and boomed, "So long everybody. Happy Christmas. Lovely pork Mrs Williams." And we heard the front door slam behind her.

"Well," said Auntie Scissors Anne. "If I live and breathe. I've never heard a voice like that in all my born days!"

Siencyn said, "It reminded me of a winter's day down the docks in Cardiff when the Fog horns was going full blast."

Dadda said, "Now listen, all the men will take the dishes into the back kitchen and do them, while the ladies have another drop of elderberry wine."

"The elderberry's all gone," said Uncle Iestyn. "Both bottles is empty, but I've opened the blackberry."

"Hang on," said Auntie Bessie. "There's no way you men could be trusted with the best china. *We'll* see to the dishes and have a sit down and a nice little drop of the blackberry wine after. Mog – where's the you-know-what?" And my new Uncle Mog, beaming like a lighthouse, produced a box of cigars!

All was bustle for a bit, then when the dishes was being done in the kitchen, the men smoking cigars in the middle room, I wandered into the from room, but wasn't wanted there neither, so I just cwtched up to Dadda on the sofa, and the smell of the cigars was beautiful.

At last, "Time to go," said Auntie Scissors Anne, so she got the coats and things. Nobody could find little Miss Williams' umbrella, but Uncle Arthur kindly said that as he was passing her house and he had a big umbrella, it didn't matter. Everybody said 'Good night' and 'Thank you,' and 'What a lovely Christmas.'

"See you all tomorrow," said Auntie Scissors Anne. "I've something for Boxing Day dinner that will surprise you," and then we were on our own.

Dadda said, "I wonder what Cissie Anne's got for us tomorrow – *ostrich?*"

Mam didn't even smile, she sighed. "I'm worn out," she said, and sat down with Dadda.

But I had a worry I had to asked about.

"Mam," I said, "If somebody do kiss you under the mistletoe, have you got to marry them?"

"No indeed," laughed Dadda. "Who've you been kissing then?"

"Cousin Billy," I said.

"No, *cariad*, you don't have to marry Cousin Billy,"

"And Uncle Arthur don't have to marry Little Miss Williams?"

"Course not," said Mam. "What put that into your head? Uncle Arthur never kissed Little Miss Williams under the mistletoe. He never kissed nobody. Shy he is."

"He did," I insisted. "Honest – when you was all washing up the supper things and the men was smoking cigars, Uncle Arthur and Little Miss Williams was in the front room by themselves tidying the music."

"I didn't put any mistletoe up in the front room," said Mam.

"Never mind mistletoe," said Auntie Bessie. "What did you see, *bach*?"

"Well," I said. "Uncle Arthur gave little Miss Williams the diamond ring from the cracker, and put it on her finger, and said he'd give her a real one as soon as the shops was open after Christmas, and Little Miss Williams said she'd treasure the cracker ring all her life, and Uncle Arthur said something about wasted years and he kissed her, so I went and sat by Dadda."

"By Jimmy Johnson!" said Dadda.

"I can't believe it," said Auntie Bessie. "Little Miss Williams and Uncle Arthur!"

"I can," said Siencyn. "They used to be sweet on each other years ago, but Uncle Arthur's father died, and he had to look after his Mam and his sister, and Little Miss Williams had her Mam ill all them years. I think there was bad feeling between the two old women too, something to do with being in charge of Sisterhood teas."

"Siencyn, why didn't you tell me?" asked Mam.

"Didn't think of it," said Siencyn. "Only just remembered, like see."

"Bed," said Dadda. "We'll talk in the morning. Perhaps there's nothing in it." But there was!

A week later, here comes Little Miss Williams and Uncle Arthur to call on us. They told us their news.

"We're engaged," they said.

Little Miss Williams showed us her ring – it didn't look a bit like the Woolworths one.

"We're getting married in February," said Uncle Arthur. "Very quiet, it will be, but you've been good to us all them years, so we would like you Mr Williams to give away the bride and Megan, to be the flower girl – no bridesmaids, only Megan, and Siencyn, will you be my best man?"

Wasn't that wonderful? Everybody looked pleased – Siencyn looked stunned! He didn't talk for two days!

Sometime later Dadda asked Uncle Arthur why he chose us to be so important in the wedding, and he said "All that long time, I've had one day a year with Mary, here in your home. Even if we didn't speak to each other, we could look at each other. Duty is a harsh and terrible thing at times, but now we're both free, and in all conscience we can be together. We are so grateful to you and your kind wife."

When Mam heard it she said that was the biggest speech she'd ever know Uncle Arthur say. "It's a real *Romeo and Juliet* story, only this one has a happy ending. Bless them both. I think I'm going to cry."

"Have my hankie," said Dadda.

I decided that if the real *Romeo and Juliet* story had a sad ending, I wouldn't read it – never ever.

Christmas had done its magic once more, everybody was happy – especially me, because I didn't have to marry Cousin Billy. I liked him, but I was going to marry Mickey Rooney when I grew up.

And Mam – well, Mam was pleased as Punch.

She'd been right all along – Uncle Arthur did want a wife!

Oh, if only it could be Christmas Day every day of the year.

THE MAN and THE WOMAN by Edwina Slack

It had been a hot day of silver sky and piercing sun – strange how I always remember the summer days, full of warmth and light, and drowsy, still afternoons. People have said to me, "A childhood in a Welsh Mining Valley during the depression – how terrible! How black and dreary it must have been," yet I always remember the sunshine, and the slate roofs of the terraced houses reflecting the sun like a mirror, and the smashed glass in the gutters brilliant as a thousand candles.

The valley slept during those hot summer afternoons. The men home from the morning shift would have bathed and taken food, and would be dozing quietly in cool, dim back kitchens. The men on the night shift would be still asleep in bed, and those on the afternoon shift would be underground in the deep dark. Old men and women would doze, mothers would rest, and the unemployed men would squat on their haunches at street corners, gazing at nothing. The children in school wished the time away.

In the early evening, the valley came alive again. Children played in the streets, old people sat outside their doors to enjoy the cooler air, while women gossiped in little groups.

I remember on that day, Gwyneth and I were playing ball. Strange how one day it would be marbles, or whip and top, or catty and doggy, then suddenly as if by a secret signal, all the children changed their games. We were playing at the corner of the street near where I lived. A line of short streets led off from the main one, and in the centre was the Grocer's shop. High up on the side of his wall was a hoarding with a poster declaring 'Out of the blue comes the whitest wash', and a smiling lady in a bright dress was hanging out sheets of vivid white which were blown by an imaginary wind against a sky blue as harebells. We liked that picture, especially as we could hit the sheets with our ball and make patterns of dusty circles on them. Gwyneth dropped the ball, it rolled into the gutter, and as I stooped to pick it up, I looked down the road and saw them: the Man and the Woman.

They were strangers – I knew that for certain. They moved uncertainly, stopped at a corner, moved on, stopped again and spoke together, and moved on once more. Despite the heat, the Man was wearing a long overcoat, and carrying a large canvas bag. The Woman was thin, and dressed in black – a black cloche hat hid her hair and most of her face, her skirt was almost ankle length, her jacket reached her knees. I watched them as they moved on again. They came to our corner, stopped and whispered together. The man nodded, and put down his bag. There were some boys playing piggy in the middle nearby. He called to them, and beckoned. They went to him, reluctantly, and stood round him, then they suddenly scattered indifferent directions.

One of the boys, Tommy Rundle, came over to Gwyneth and me. "That man told us we've got to go home and get our mothers and fathers to come out by here and watch him because he's going to do tricks and juggling and things. He said get as many people as you can." He raced off, slapping his thighs, pretending to be galloping a fast horse.

"I'm not going to," I said. I knew my mother was putting by baby brother to bed, and my father was out, but I did not like the idea, somehow. Gwyneth had no misgivings; she ran indoors and called her mother. The people came out of their houses, one or two at first, then more and more people converged on the corner, until a small crowd had gathered. They were shy, awkward, embarrassed. They whispered together, "What's it all about?"

"No idea."

"What's happening?"

I stood by Gwyneth and her mother. Some girls ran up and stood in front of me, but I didn't care. I was uneasy and I didn't know why. Tiny fingers of vague fear were moving inside my head. I watched, but said nothing.

The Woman leaned against the wall of Becca Thomas's house. Her face was ashen, her eyes fixed on the ground. She bent her head, and the hat hid all but her trembling lips. She seemed to be trying to merge into the stones of the house, to disappear from what was happening, to shrink into the wall. In her hand she held the man's cloth cap. I knew what that meant – I had seen it so many times. They had come to beg money, and her shame was suffocating her.

The Man took off his long, shabby overcoat. There was a gasp from the little crowd – the Man was naked from the waist upwards. His body was smooth and brown and shining like silk. I had never seen such naked flesh before. I had seen men stripped to the waist, carrying loads of coal into their coal houses from the back lanes where it had been dumped by the pit lorries, but their flesh was white, blue scarred and vulnerable, with hair sprouting from their chests. This was a different nakedness, slim-waisted, tight-muscled, a nakedness that had been groomed and cared for. He wore navy blue serge trousers, shiny and well worn, but trim and well fitting. His feet were bare, slim and delicate-boned, yet hard and strong.

He beckoned the crowd to come nearer. A few children moved forward, glancing round uncertainly, then sheepishly moving back. In silence we stared across the gap between the corner where the uneasy crowd stood. The Man took some dumbbells from the bag. He lay down on his back on the coat, held the dumbbells in his hands, then with a deft throw, he caught them with his feet. He made them spin and turn and twist in the air. He took other things from his bag, sticks, balls, a bar with a ball at each end, and all these in turn were flicked into the air and made to dance, to balance, to fly. There was no sound from the crowd, the Man or the Woman. No train passed noisily along the nearby siding, no dog barked, no distant bus chugged along the Main Road. It was all wrong. I knew it was wrong, but I could not understand why. I know now there should have been lights and sequins and rich coloured satins and drums and cymbals, and an audience lost in the magic of the theatre. I did not know it then. I stopped looking at the Man. I stared at the back of the girl who stood in front of me. I saw the pattern of rosebuds on her dress, the material faded except where the waistband had been torn and the original bright colours were still visible. I saw the buttons - five original, and one that had been replaced and did not match the others - and the neat patch where the pattern did not fit. I stared at the rosebuds until my eyes began to swim. I counted the rosebuds over and over again, four pink upright ones, two rosebuds upside down, four rosebuds the right way up. Over and over, I counted the rosebuds while the performance seemed to take up the whole of time.

There was a slight movement in the crowd. I looked up. The Man was on his feet, bowing to left and right. A few people clapped. The applause was thin and feeble. The Man took his cap from the Woman's hands, and put it on the ground. A few people, awkward and embarrassed, stepped forward and put a few coins in the cap. The Woman hid her face against the wall. The children went off to play; in twos and threes the crowd moved off. I stood with Gwyneth and her mother and watched while the Man put away the dumbbells and the sticks, and put on his coat and shoes. A small group of people still stood on the corner, whispering together. Ceinwen, who lived opposite us, and her husband were among them. Suddenly she left the group, and went over to the Man, and started to talk to him. After a short while, she turned and beckoned her husband to join her. A few minutes later, Ceinwen took the Woman's hand, and gently led her away from the corner, down the street to her own house. The Man followed, and went inside. Ceinwen's husband went over to the few people left spoke to them, then they all followed him across the road and into the house. The front door was shut, and the brass knocker jumped and went tut-tut-tuttuttut.

Suddenly, I could bear no more. "I'm going home," I said to Gwyneth, and ran off. I wanted to forget what I had seen. I couldn't understand why it had upset and depressed me. I went through the back lane gate, into the small paved yard, and into the kitchen. It was always dark in the kitchen. The window looked out onto the wall of the house next door, which was only a few feet away. My mother was sitting by the table, her arm resting on the arm of her chair, her forehead resting on her hand. She did not look up as I came in.

"Don't make a noise, I've just got the baby off to sleep," she said. "Your supper's ready."

I washed my hands at the tap in the lean to glasshouse, then picked up my library book from the dresser. I sat at the table. My supper was on a plate, two pieces of bread and butter with slices of tomato. The other half of the tomato lay, cut side down, on a plate ready for my mother's supper. I opened my library book, propped it against the teapot and read as I ate. I loved that book, Andrew Lang's Olive Fairy Book. I loved the stories where magic was the norm, and good always triumphed and princesses married paupers and goose girls married princes. The illustrations were beautiful. I know now that they were Art Nouveau, but then all I knew was that their beauty captivated me. Despite the silence in the house, I read on; I read on even when my father came home and sat on a chair by the empty grate. Not a word passed between any of us.

There was a knock on the front door. My mother did not move. With an impatient exclamation, my father got up and went to see who it was. I heard voices, then my father saying, "You'd better come in then," and my father came back with our next door neighbour.

"It's Mr Watkins," he said. "Sit down and tell us what it's all about then."

And then I heard the story of the Man and the Woman, how they were respectable people from the top of the Valley, had a nice business, then their son was hurt in the pit and no compensation, then the struggle to live had turned to debts and now, that day, they had literally no food in the house, and no money or the likelihood of getting any. They were desperate, but were afraid of letting their neighbours know. They decided to use the Man's skill at juggling to earn something – it seems he used to perform at charity concerts, and taught Keep Fit at Boy's Clubs, and Clubs for the unemployed. They were ashamed because instead of being someone who helped the poor, they had become part of the Poor themselves. They had walked miles down the Valley – Tylorstown, Porth Trehafod, looking for somewhere where they would not be recognised. They could not bear that their neighbours might know about their desperate situation. This was the first time the Man had performed at a street corner to beg for money, and they experience had smashed their self-respect. Ceinwen had taken them in and was giving them a good supper. Other women in the neighbourhood were giving food for them to take home with them, and some of the men were going round the houses to collect money for them. Mr Watkins showed my father the brown paper fruit bag a quarter full of coppers. He asked if he would care to contribute.

My father stood up. "God dammit," he shouted. "What does this bloody government think it's doing when good, respectable, hardworking people are put to shame like this? The way things are going, this could happen to anybody. It could be your wife, or mine, begging in the streets like this."

I felt a stab of pain. The words jangled and echoed in my head. "Your wife, or mine – or mine – or mine." I looked at my mother. She had not moved, not even when our neighbour had come in. Her face was pale and thin. I know now it was lack of sleep, a poor confinement, lack of nourishment and the endless vista of the years of unemployment for my father that had worn her down, but I did not understand that then. I saw in my mind's eye the Woman shrinking against the wall, the begging cap held in her hands. The woman's face blurred and became my mother's face, vulnerable before the blank stare of the crowd. I was too frightened to move, or cry, or show I had heard.

"Here," said my father. "Here's all I got. I wish I could give more." He held out three pennies.

"Lovely," said Mr Watkins. "Very good of you. It's coming in – copper mostly – but it'll all add up. Well. I'll be going, got a lot more houses to go to."

"I'll see you to the door," said my father. I heard the sound of the front door closing, then my father came back into the kitchen. "Poor devils," he said. "This ruddy government ought to come down here and see what's happening, see how people are suffering." My mother moved her hand from her forehead and looked at him.

"Why did you have to give him all that money?" she asked. "Three whole pence! I've got nothing left for the rest of the week and you lord it and give all that to these people. Think of your own wife and children first – we need it as much as they do. I could have bought three pennorth of beef pieces with that money – two dinners I could have made, but you put strangers before us."

My father began to shout. "Damn it all, can't I help somebody in trouble without you going on at me?" He snatched up his cap and made for the door.

"Where are you going?" asked my mother. "Out!" he shouted, and the door slammed behind him. The awful silence settled like deadening snow on the house again.

My mother hid her face in her hands. I tried to read, but the words jumbled and ran into each other. The silence grew until I felt paralysed.

At last, without looking up, my mother said, "Time for bed." Obediently I rose, put my book on the dresser and went to the glass house. I filled the bowl with cold water and washed quietly, without splashing, afraid to break the dreadful quiet. I folded my clothes carefully. I made sure I was clean, all the dirt and sweat of the hot day cleared by the cold water and rough flannel and harsh green soap. I cleaned my teeth with salt, and gargled my throat with salt and water. As I had been taught, I put away the bowl, tidied the sink and spread the coarse canvas towel to dry.

I went back into the kitchen. My mother was sitting exactly as before. The room was beginning to darken even further with the sunset, and my mother's face was in shadow. I walked past her to the dresser for my book.

"No reading in bed tonight," she said. "It's dark, you'll strain your eyes."

It was out of the question to have a candle just to read by in bed; a candle cost a halfpenny. Sadly, I put my book down. I was in need of its comfort, but the habit of obedience could not be broken. I walked to the door leading to the stairs. I looked back at the withdrawn figure of my mother.

"Night, night," I said.

Without moving, she answered me. "Night, night."

Quietly I went upstairs. In my parents' room, my little brother was sleeping. My bare feet made no sound as I passed the door.

In my bedroom, it was still hot even though the window was opened at the top and bottom. The setting sun shining through the threadbare curtains made patterns of wavy lines on the wall. I put my clothes neatly on the chair by the window, where my school clothes were all ready for the morning. I said my prayers, and got into bed. The street was quiet. From a distance I heard the shunting of coal trucks on the railway. Far off, a dog barked.

I lay for a long time unable to sleep, then I heard the sound of Ceinwen's door knocker, tut, tut, tut-tut-tut, and voices. I got out of bed and moved quietly to the window. Our house was exactly opposite, so I could see clearly. Ceinwen's husband was standing on the pavement. He was carrying a brown paper fish frail. The Man and the Woman came out of the house. They were carrying bags and parcels. Ceinwen stood on the doorstep. They spoke quietly, then the Man and the Woman shook hands with Ceinwen, and they set off down the street with Cienwen's husband. Ceinwen watched them go. Another woman who had been standing her own door to enjoy the last of the evening's cool air, went over to Cienwen. I heard, "He's going to send them to the bus."

By now, the Man and the Woman had reached the end of the street. They turned, waved, and were gone. I heard Ceinwen say, "Come in a minute," and the two women went into the house, and the door was shut. The sound of the knocker jumping up and down was like an Amen. The episode was over. The Man and the Woman had come into our lives, and had gone. The chapter had lasted a few hours, and was now closed – or was it?

I got back into bed. The room darkened, and a slight breeze stirred the curtains. I lay in the silent house in a loneliness that was almost tangible. I knew now that my cocoon of childhood was smashed, that there was no security, that our way of life was a fragile tightrope that could snap and send us hurtling down. I did not think then of the way two strangers had been helped by people who were themselves poor, but generous. It is only now that I see hope and love in this small incident. When it happened, I only knew that the coming of the Man and the Woman into my life had brought desolation too deep for tears, because I understood my mother's despair.

Printed in Great Britain
by Amazon

65975842R00104